INTO THE SILENCE

INTO THE SILENCE

✦

The Power of Stillness
in Living and Dying

Judith M. Ashley

iUniverse, Inc.

New York Lincoln Shanghai

INTO THE SILENCE
The Power of Stillness in Living and Dying

iUniverse books may be ordered through booksellers or by contacting:

iUniverse
2021 Pine Lake Road, Suite 100
Lincoln, NE 68512
www.iuniverse.com
1-800-Authors (1-800-288-4677)

Because of the dynamic nature of the Internet, any Web addresses
or links contained in this book may have changed
since publication and may no longer be valid.

The views expressed in this work are solely those of the author and do not necessarily reflect the views of the publisher, and the publisher hereby disclaims any responsibility for them.

Cover photograph by Brad Markel

ISBN: 978-0-595-44085-6 (pbk)
ISBN: 978-0-595-68900-2 (cloth)
ISBN: 978-0-595-88408-7 (ebk)

Printed in the United States of America

In honor of
Enid Louise

O Fly, my Soul! What hangs upon
  Thy drooping wings,
    And weighs them down
With love of gaudy mortal things?

The Sun is now i' the east: each shade
    As he doth rise
      Is shorter made,
That earth may lessen to our eyes.

—James Shirley, *A Hymn*, 1596–1666

Contents

Enid aged 16

Preface

Thirty one years prior to the time this book covers, my first husband and I immigrated to the United States with our three young children. Six years passed before I returned to England to visit my parents, and thereafter I tried to do so once a year, for seven days or so—frequently enough to hold mutual love and respect for one another, but insufficient time to develop a more substantive relationship. After my father died, these short annual visits continued—to see my mother.

My visits were fleeting days of pleasure, packed with activity, but little depth of relationship. The latter was not to develop fully until the last weeks of my mother's life, when during one of our frequent, transatlantic phone calls, I heard her say these words: "The doctor says it's time for you to come." It was then, when I went to care for her until her death, that our intimacy deepened, and our relationship unfolded in amazing ways.

While I prepared to leave my home in New Mexico, to care for my mother in England during her final weeks, I was aware of a persistent and distracting thought ticking away in my mind. How could I support my mother fully, yet still honor my own need to remain intimately connected with my second husband, HB? Being apart from him was inevitable, mutually undesirable and unavoidable.

We had married less than eight years earlier, and enjoyed a deep, intimate bond of friendship, and an unconditional acceptance of one another—absent in our former marriages. HB, seven years my senior, was diagnosed with malignant melanoma soon after our wedding and, following hastily scheduled surgery, he retired from his career of consulting for manufacturing start-ups to focus on two things: building his immune system, and spending as much time together as possible.

My work, as a human resources consultant in a high tech corporation, took me all over the world, however, and away from him on a regular basis. We cherished our time together and here I was, leaving again; we knew not for how long.

On the way to the airport we agreed, that while apart, we would nurture ourselves and one another, by talking regularly by phone, and corresponding, in writing, as frequently as possible.

The day after I arrived at my mother's home to care for her, and during the ensuing days and weeks, I wrote home of many things. Writing to HB, once, twice, and sometimes three times a day, provided unexpected gifts. The *act* of writing became a portal to a stillness within, from which I observed each moment of my mother's last weeks—and my own way of being—as I tended to her needs. All that I felt, thought, and witnessed, poured into my letters.

Several years later, when HB came across those letters again, I went through them one-by-one and was moved to share—with anyone who has ever loved—the conscious way in which my mother approached the last year of her life, and my intensely personal experience of it. In so doing, my intention is to illuminate the *power of stillness* available to each of us, not only in the face of death, but throughout our everyday life.

Herewith, in all humility, I share those letters and my dear mother, Enid, with you.

—Judith M. Ashley
June, 2007

Acknowledgments

Thanks to my editor, Cecelia Cancellaro, whose encouragement and expertise were invaluable; to Tom Davison and Diane Pitochelli, who gave unstinting feedback on the first draft of the manuscript; to Nicole Barde, who allowed me re-acclimation time when it was needed most; to Sándor, Anna and David, whose love reached across the miles; to my sister, Ann, deepest gratitude and love, for the constancy of support for our mother, especially during her own such challenging years; to my brothers, Damian and Kevin, who, by their presence, brought such happiness to our mother's last days; to Hazel, Rachel, and Dr. R. Ashman, for their tender administrations, and to HB—for being on this journey together.

Introduction

My siblings and I spent several years of our childhood living on the coast of Somerset, in England, at the hotel my parents bought soon after the end of the Second World War. After owning and operating this small business for several years, my father sold it and they retired to Cornwall. By then my siblings and I had left home, and we were out in the world of work.

Over the next fifteen years, during which I emigrated from England to the USA, my parents moved three times and, at the age of seventy-two, without prior ill-health, my father died of a massive heart attack. At the time of his death, my mother, Enid, was sixty-five.

During their marriage my father controlled the household and business finances, and when he died, Mother had no inkling of her financial status. After a rapid acclimatization to her unexpected widowhood, and the disastrous discovery that there was a virtually empty bank account and no life insurance, my mother turned to my sister, Ann, for counsel. At that time Ann lived twenty or so miles from Mother's home, and she willingly began to tutor Mother on the ins and outs of managing household accounts.

It soon became evident that Mother must sell her home—not in the least reluctantly, as my father had chosen it for them—and she reinvested a portion of the proceeds in a smaller, charming, older home with low beamed ceilings and a fireplace. She saved the remainder of the proceeds to supplement her government pension, and continued adjusting to living her life alone; an unfamiliar experience to say the least.

Prompted by my father's sudden death, I wrote to ask my mother how she wanted to be cared for in her later years if, unlike her husband, she was able to exercise a choice. After some weeks her reply came: "Thank you for asking, dear. If I become senile, I want you all (her children) to sell my home and use the money to put me in a nursing home, where I can hide away and die quietly in complete privacy. I wouldn't want anyone to see me that way. But if I am not senile, I would prefer to die at home in my own bed."

As I read her letter I vowed to honor her wishes and wrote to affirm my promise.

◆   ◆   ◆

Nine years later, Mother was diagnosed with chronic leukemia, which debilitated her health but certainly not her interest in life. Eleven years on, when she was diagnosed with cancer, the opportunity to follow through on my promise arrived.

I was by her hospital bed when the surgeon gave her a prognosis of "… about a year." As he left her side, Mother turned to me and, looking directly into my eyes, she reached gently for my hand and set in motion what was to come, by saying, with such simplicity, "Judith, I'm going to need your help."

And thus the fulfillment of my promise began.

1

Sanctuary

At eighty-three, my mother had certainly lived a long life, yet we hadn't imagined that her recent visit to our home was to be her last.

A year prior, I, and my second husband, HB, and Ollie, our golden retriever, moved into a modest adobe home on a couple of acres of land in the northern foothills of the Sandia Mountains, in central New Mexico. When we moved in, the area immediately behind the house was no more than a scrubby, desert sand lot, littered with tumbleweed and dog feces.

We spent the first year transforming the area around the house into a courtyard, enclosed by an undulating, straw-bale wall. The garden within the courtyard was designed and planted to attract butterflies and birds. A small pond, with a cascading mushroom fountain, became the central feature, the gliding black moors and golden fantails occasionally visible in the shadows of the lily pads. Flagstones formed a meandering path around sweetly-scented desert shrubs and soft-hued flowers, among them, purple Liatris, Russian sage, Mexican hat, and chocolate flowers. An inviting garden bench was positioned in the shade of mountain cottonwoods.

Two gates were built into the straw-bale wall. One, facing north, led yonder to the wildflower garden, bird feeders and nesting boxes; the other, facing east, opened onto the vegetable and sunflower gardens. We called this home Sanctuary, and it was to this place that Mother came for her long-planned vacation.

During her stay in the late spring and early summer, pain and discomfort accompanied many of her waking hours, though she said nothing about it overtly, and did not allow it to dim her joy at being with us. Though she was coping with chronic leukemia for the prior nine years—and other ailments, of which she rarely spoke—she continued to look her best by dressing in her usual style: pencil-slim skirt, form-fitting, long-sleeved blouse, nylon stockings, and high-heeled shoes.

I'd notice her sitting with her hands gently nursing her abdomen, one foot in constant motion, as though to distract her. She took medication several times a day telling us it was for diverticulitis. She wouldn't hear of shortening her vacation to seek care from her doctor in England; neither would she allow us to take her for local medical attention. "It will pass soon enough," she'd say, and change the subject. She was determined to be with us for the full ten weeks she had planned.

Respecting her wishes, we showered her with gentle care, serving her appetizing portions of her favorite foods; taking short drives into the high mesas; sitting quietly, in the shaded warmth and silence of the courtyard; providing soothing foot massages; soft music, and fresh flowers in her room. HB and I did whatever we could to nurture her.

On peacefully still afternoons, with Ollie at her side, Mother would recline on a comfy chaise in the shade of the north-facing patio, inhaling the fragrance of the sage and chocolate flowers. Her deep sighs of contentment were audible through the screened window.

The soft cascade of the fountain lulled her to sleep, and the occasional splashes of the golden fantails, or the whir of hummingbirds as they drank from the scarlet penstemons, woke her with a start, but always smiling. She told me later that the view to the horizon, seventy miles distant over sprawling, far-reaching mesas, afforded her the emotional sanctuary she sought, in which to reflect on her life—and as she alone already knew—on her impending death.

She was to reluctantly acknowledge, later, seeing blood in her feces (perhaps over a period of several years, according to my sister's strong suspicions), yet Mother chose to withhold this information from her doctor, not wanting him to exert any influence on her choice to allow whatever was going on in her body to run its course, or on her long-planned vacation. She knew she had cancer, and later told me, "I welcome death as much as life." She never seemed afraid.

Two weeks after I accompanied Mother back to her home in the southwest of England, and returned alone to New Mexico, I received an urgent call from my sister, Ann, saying that Mother, in extreme pain, had called her. Ann phoned the doctor immediately; he arrived within half an hour, and after a cursory examination and over Mother's protests, he quickly summoned an ambulance. Mother refused to be carried to the ambulance on a stretcher. "I can still walk under my own steam," she quipped, and with head held high she climbed in unaided. As Ann recounted, the only hint of alarm—though her demeanor denied it—was the wary expression in Mother's gentle, blue eyes.

Mother, in the Sanctuary garden

I quickly arranged for a "Family Medical Leave of Absence" from work, and flew to England two days later. While waiting for test results to come in, and for her current condition to stabilize, a surgeon gave Mother his considered opinion—the need for major surgery, scheduled two days hence, and her chances of surviving it. Without any visible emotion Mother relayed his words to me, "He says I have a fifty-fifty chance of coming out of surgery. If I do, will you be here?" I assured her that I would.

Three days after admission, Mother was wheeled from the operating room on a gurney festooned with inverted bottles, tubes leading to her inert body. Her surgeon followed, sliding his green cap into his hand as he paced down the corridor towards me. He stopped, looked into my eyes, and said wearily, "Your mother has cancer of the bowel and liver; I couldn't get it all, but she came through it well."

I felt a chill move down my spine and reminded myself to breathe. Inhaling deeply, I expressed my thanks for his work and hurried to Mother's bedside.

The ward had eight beds, all occupied. A nurse sat at a table at the head of the ward, engrossed in paperwork lit by a bright desk lamp; all other lights were dimmed. I took a seat behind the curtains drawn around Mother's bed and waited in silence.

After three long, anxious hours Mother woke sufficiently to ask in a dreamy voice, "Am I alive?"

"Yes, you're alive," I replied, gently smoothing her brow.

"Well, *that's* a surprise."

A moment later she groaned in pain. "I feel horrible. Come back in the morning, will you, dear?"

Kissing her forehead softly, I whispered, "I love you, Mother," and, signaling to the nurse that I was leaving, I tiptoed away. Driving back to her home, thirty miles away, I felt deep gratitude for her deliverance from surgery and, at the same time, a tearful dread of the predicted conclusion.

The following morning, at Mother's request, I remained at her bedside when the surgeon came on his rounds. Mother addressed him forthrightly, "How long do I have, Doctor?" She never minced her words.

"Your liver is involved. We couldn't get it all. I'd say you have about twelve months."

Smiling up at him with great charm, Mother inclined her head, "Thank you, Doctor." She was always charming, always calm, and always gracious. It was mid-July.

She was discharged ten days later and taken by ambulance to a small hospital in her home town, where a week's convalescence was arranged by her doctor. I drove ahead and met the ambulance as it pulled into the gravel driveway. Aided by an attendant, Mother stepped down dressed in the clothes she had asked me to bring her for the journey: a slim brown skirt, silk blouse, a scarf tucked around her neck, nylon stockings and high heels. She insisted on walking from the ambulance into the hospital and, with our arms linked, we crossed the stone threshold into a cavernous hall.

Greeted by a nurse, who was clearly expecting her, Mother was admitted to a ward on the first floor. As I put her toiletry items into the small cabinet beside her assigned bed, Mother looked around the ward with some trepidation. No aesthetics here—all surfaces painted white; floor waxed to a high sheen; taut, white linen on all six beds, and no flowers in sight. The lack of privacy would not be any easier for her here than at the prior hospital.

"Let's go and see what else is here," she said purposefully, and linking her arm in mine, we headed in the direction of the solarium.

The solarium housed several elderly women dressed in long, cotton night-gowns. Shawls or cardigans hung carelessly around their shoulders and slippers hugged their feet. They looked tired, their hair unkempt. Listless and silent, they sat around the perimeter of the room, pale-faced and slack-mouthed, some drooling, their vacant, rheumy eyes fixed on the television. A game show was in progress, the volume turned down low, almost inaudible; no one looked up as we entered.

Mother absorbed the entire sad scene then taking a deep breath she squeezed my arm gently and slowly turned us around. We walked quietly out into the corridor, where she hugged my arm closer to her side and whispered, conspiratorially, "I'm not staying here dear. Everyone is old and sick! I don't belong in this place!"

Urgently, I whispered back, "Your doctor has arranged for you to convalesce here for a week!"

"I know that. But I'm *not* staying. When you've only got fifty left, a week is a week."

I coaxed her gently, "Ask the doctor when he comes in. See what he advises."

"Oh, I shall!" She gave me a knowing look, which I could not quite interpret.

As I helped her to change into her nightgown and bed jacket I kept calm by breathing evenly and deeply. When I left her she was in bed, propped up with pillows, reading a Dick Francis novel. She looked beautiful, her curly hair, still ash-blond and sprinkled with silver at the temples, framed her lovely, classic features; her shoulders were covered with a cream-colored, knitted bed jacket, neatly buttoned to the throat, the neckline chosen carefully to hide her thin, scrawny neck—her modesty and vanity, as always, hand-in-hand.

The next morning at 9:00 AM, a call came from the local hospital. A woman's cheerful voice informed me, "Doctor has discharged your mother. Will you come and pick her up right away? She is *most* anxious to leave."

As soon as her luggage was loaded into the trunk and we were safely buckled in, I turned to her with admiration and curiosity. "Mother, how *did* you manage to escape?"

She smiled mischievously, "Well, when Doctor came in I told him I didn't belong there at all. Not for *one* more minute. I told him, I'm not old and I'm not sick. Then I asked him what I needed to do to get back to my own home."

Marveling at her determination I sat quietly with her hand resting in mine; she continued, "He said that as I have stairs at home, he wanted me to stay in the hospital until I could go up and down the stairs safely, by myself. He said he thought that in about a week I might be strong enough to do it. So I asked him if he could wait for just a minute while I called the nurse." She gave a little smile as she related the doctor's nodding response. "I rang the bell for the nurse, who

came immediately. I asked her to please take me to the stairs, and I suppose …"
Mother paused, "I suppose she needed Doctor's permission, because she looked
at him with her eyebrows raised; I was worried for a moment, but when I saw
Doctor nodding again, I asked the nurse to walk beside me but not to help me at
all." At this, she squeezed my hand and, dimpling with delight, added, "Then I
hauled myself to the top of the stairs and down again—quite unaided." A chuckle
escaped her as she added in a low conspiratorial tone, "I don't know if the doctor
noticed but I was holding on to the banisters for dear life." Then, as if she had
pulled off a great coup, she said, "What else *could* he do but discharge me?" She
squeezed my hand, harder this time. "I was *determined* to get out of there. I want
to get on with my life *and* death, from the sanctuary of my own home."

As we pulled out of the parking lot and headed for home she looked straight
ahead, her eyes bright with victory. I just caught her barely audible words, said
firmly to herself, "I shall be alright now."

I was aware of some anxiety, rising like a cloying mist, as the inevitable need
for her care loomed. This was unexplored territory. How could she manage? Who
would care for her?

◆   ◆   ◆

She was born in the Midlands, in the town of Erdington, the first child of
middle class parents of English, Scots, and Welsh heritage; she was named Enid
Louise.

Her father, Will, was an accomplished water-colorist and pianist, which he
practiced for his own amusement. He stood a slim, five feet four, his eyes a pierc-
ing blue, his brow straight, his cheek bones high, his chin small and aggressive.
He sported a neatly trimmed moustache, which he would absentmindedly
smooth with thumb and forefinger when he laughed, spreading his digits apart
across its width. Despite his diminutive stature, he stood tall, holding his back
ramrod straight.

My grandmother, Norah, stood five feet two, with laughing blue eyes, round,
rosy cheeks and a constant chuckle, deep and warm. She and Will enjoyed the
happiest of marriages. After their death, my mother conjectured that they would
have been just as happy without children. "They lived in a world unto themselves," she would say wistfully, exposing tender feelings of exclusion.

When Enid was 2 years old, her brother, Keith, was born. To her disappointment—and lifelong resentment—her solitary world of creative playtime was
abruptly interrupted by the demanding responsibility placed upon her by her

mother, to attend to Keith's every whim. Notwithstanding her resentment, Enid became an obedient and dutiful child.

At sixteen, she converted to Roman Catholicism, the only one of her family to do so at that time. During that same year, she attended the local art school, where she explored her inherited artistic talent and dreamed of contributing to the world of haute couture. To her dismay, however, her father withdrew her from school to take fulltime care of her twin, newborn sisters, with whom my grandmother could not cope alone. Despite more smoldering resentment, Enid held her silence on the subject—at that time.

At eighteen, soon after she met and fell in love with Phil, later to become my father, she outwitted her parent's expectations of her by accepting the position of governess to two young girls—Nena Mina and Lola—the daughters of a wealthy Spanish family, who lived in Santander, on the coast of Spain.

Enid loved her young charges. In fact, she developed a lifelong love for everything Spanish: the lyrical language; the ornate architecture with its classic interiors; the luscious colors and textures, and the rich culture, with its spirited music—including the sensual flamenco.

On the seemingly endless sunny, summer days, Enid taught English to the girls in the morning and they spent playful afternoons together at the beach. She was happy to be free of her demanding parents and siblings. While there, she and Phil stayed in touch, sending each other recent photographs and writing letters, regularly.

On a visit to see her, about a year after she went to Spain, Phil, my father-to-be, suspecting Enid might otherwise succumb to the advances of an amorous, handsome Spaniard, proposed. They married when she was twenty, and Phil, twenty-eight, and they moved into a three-bedroom home—chosen by Phil before Enid returned from Spain—near Sutton Coldfield, in the Midlands.

I was born, the youngest of four, when Enid was only twenty-six, by which time she was happily engaged in her duties as an obedient wife and loving mother.

Though shy and modest, Enid was meticulous about her appearance and that of her children. She had her father's blue eyes, classic, high cheek bones, and a delicate jaw. Her baby-fine hair was ash-blonde and curly; her mouth, generous and full. By all accounts, and I remember many such occasions, those who saw her with her four young children were compelled to stop and comment on her beauty, and that of her young family. Like Enid, each of us had a fair complexion, curly hair and blue eyes—the stereotypical English ideal of beauty, then.

Young Enid was proud of her growing family. Indeed, it was her home and family that were of the highest value to her throughout her life, though she was not to clarify this until she was eighty-four.

◆　　　◆　　　◆

Within a day or two of escaping from the planned week's convalescence at the local hospital, Mother and her doctor set about identifying some affordable home care for her. In the meantime, I stayed with her for two more weeks, taking care of her day-to-day needs while she recuperated. During that time I asked her to think about how I could help her, once I returned home to New Mexico. Living so far away I wasn't sure what I could do, but sure enough, just before I left, she clearly defined the help she wanted me to provide, by saying, "I'd like you to help me sort everything out. You know, help me work out what I need to do before I die. Ask me the tough questions. You're good at that." She paused before imploring, "And Judith, *please* be with me at the end."

I agreed immediately, feeling deeply privileged and humbled by her request. And just as quickly, I noticed a knot of fear in my stomach. Was I up to this?

By the time I returned to New Mexico, Mother was in good hands. Her doctor had arranged for professional caregivers to come to her home three times a week and it was already working well, despite Mother's voiced concern about how she would cope with strangers coming into her home, "I shouldn't *need* any help. I don't want to be a bother to anyone. It's really best if I do everything myself, I have my *own* way of doing things."

On their designated days, the caregivers, either Hazel or Rachel, arrived to help her; I liked them both instantly. Hazel, a peppery brunette in her mid-thirties, little more than five feet tall, is round-faced, with serious, yet kind, hazel eyes. The mother of teenagers, she seemed pragmatic, with warmth of personality I found comforting. Rachel, who always seemed light-hearted, is younger and taller than Hazel, with deep velvet-brown eyes, shining dark hair to her shoulders, and a sparkling personality. She and Hazel complemented each other well, and I discovered they were good friends as well as professional colleagues.

On their visits, either Hazel or Rachel would bathe Mother and take her breakfast in bed. After washing the dishes, a pre-packaged, nutritiously-balanced meal—ordered fourteen-to-the-case from a meal-delivery service—was taken from the freezer to thaw, ready for Mother to heat for lunch. These caring women changed the bed and bath linens, took care of the laundry, and did the grocery shopping.

Mother quickly grew to love them. They were always prompt, cheerful, and gentle. They were extremely efficient, yet never seemed rushed; over a cup of tea or coffee they always made time for a chat with her, before moving on to their next client. It was clear that they were sincerely interested in Mother's well-being and comfort; when they were with her, Mother seemed to be the only one in the world they had to care for. She loved their kind attention and "pampering," as she called it.

While still ambulatory, Mother insisted on doing whatever she could manage alone. This included dressing herself, her evening ablutions and, on the days her caregivers were elsewhere, preparing her own meals. On one occasion, after I had left but still in the early weeks following her surgery, she was determined to walk the quarter mile to the village for fresh vegetables, meat, and cut flowers. Completely exhausted by the effort, she needed a taxi to take her home. That was the last day the grocer, the butcher, and the florist saw her. She could not summon the strength or will to do it again.

She dusted her oak furniture every day and, as she could no longer carry the vacuum cleaner up and down stairs, she carefully budgeted to hire a local woman to come in once a month, for two hours, to help with the heavy cleaning. Mother's home was always immaculate, and the fact that she was dying did nothing to change her determination to keep it that way. She managed her meager income well enough to allow weekly visits from her hairdresser. Looking her best at all times was of the utmost importance to her, right up until the end. During those last months, the structure of her daily life brought her comfort. Domesticity and self-care were familiar. Dying was not.

For the next nine months our former weekly phone calls became daily forty-five minute conversations. No matter where my work took me—whether to Oregon, Massachusetts, California, Israel, or Malaysia—I placed a daily call to her at noon Greenwich Mean Time. This was how I could support her, by staying in close touch, by making the time to help her identify what she wanted to do to prepare for death, and by listening deeply—even to her long silences—as she pondered a question I posed.

Mother emphasized that she wanted to leave *nothing* undone. When I asked her to explain further, she said she wanted to have everything taken care of, so that her life would feel uncluttered when it came close to the end. "So I can relax into death, without worrying about leaving a muddle behind for *you* to sort out."

Over the ensuing weeks she identified many, many tasks that needed her attention, and she pursued the process of completing them with gusto.

Perhaps with as much gusto as she had felt soon after the start of the Second World War, when my father hurried his young wife and family to a rural village hide-away, in Ryton, in the county of Shropshire, on the border of England and Wales. He wanted us to be in a safe haven, away from the bombing raids on the Midlands, where he and my mother had their first home. I recall my father speaking of the enthusiasm Mother showed for that particular move.

◆   ◆   ◆

In Ryton, our leased thatched cottage on the edge of the village was surrounded by a vast, unkempt garden: the neglected lawns were bordered by overgrown beds of red poppies and blue cornflowers; tall nettles formed a backdrop against two stone walls and another was fronted by untamed rose bushes. Clumps of yews provided ideal hiding places for Enid's four young children and in late summer the fruit trees yielded warm windfalls—to the delight of those of us still too small to reach the lowest branches.

Opposite the cottage was a working farm. I fondly recall lying in my crib listening to the bellowing of the resident bull, his booming call drowning out the lowing of cows during the morning milking in the dairy barn. Occasionally, to the alarm of my brothers, sister and I, we heard the squealing of a pig as it raced frantically around the cobbled farmyard, trying to escape the butcher's knife held by the chasing farmer. Once, we climbed the five-barred gate and, with fingers pressed into our ears, we watched the slaughter with bugging eyes.

Our cottage had no interior plumbing, though there were four outhouses down the garden away from the house—each with its own door. The well-pump was close to the back door, and young Enid would draw off clear, cold, spring water, to be heated for washing dishes and clothes, scouring pans, and bathing her four youngsters in the tin tub, before the fire, on Saturday nights.

In later years, Mother would talk wistfully of our time at the cottage in Ryton. With deep conviction she would say, "Those were the *happiest* days of my life, when I was left to my own devices without your father's needs to attend to, and I could focus solely on you children and the way *I* wanted to bring you up."

Though my father served in the Home Guard, his profession exempted him from overseas military service, and also absented him from home on weekdays. Thus from Monday to Friday, Mother could set her own boundaries regarding our behavior, and spent those days as she preferred, caring for the four of us in her pastoral haven.

We lived at the cottage for two and a half years, until the air raids subsided and the roof of our bombed town home was replaced. V-E Day was drawing in—just as my mother's death was, now.

◆   ◆   ◆

And here was Mother, on another of our noon phone conversations, telling me with great enthusiasm about reorganizing her files, which she'd completed while relaxing in her favorite armchair and watching horse racing on television. She loved horse racing. My father, who was a Saturday gambler, introduced Mother to the sport early in their marriage. She held no interest in betting, only in the glorious spectacle of the event.

I listened, as she told me how she'd placed her file boxes on a small table beside her chair and between televised races she'd gone methodically through each box, until she completed A—Z. On another call she reported, "So much rubbish sorted out and thrown away. It feels marvelous!" Another time, a triumphant smile evident in her voice, she told me, "All those envelopes of photos that have overstuffed my desk drawer for years, I've sorted through them all! The best ones are now in albums, with notations, and in chronological order. I threw the rest away! It took me a whole month. You'll have to fight over who gets which ones!"

Fighting with my three siblings over photographs was the farthest thing from my mind.

For most of her adult life my mother weighed no more than ninety-five pounds, and at five feet two inches tall and eighty-three years of age, though her abdomen was swelling with an invading malignancy, her slim figure was still in perfect proportion. She was beautiful. Admired throughout her adult life by men and women alike, she enjoyed attention—though with lifelong self-effacement.

She chose her elegant size four, and perfectly coordinated clothing for its quality, muted colors and classic design. She cared for her wardrobe meticulously. "They have to last you know," she'd say with a twinkle in her eye, reminiscent of her natural frugality, heightened no doubt during and after WWII.

◆   ◆   ◆

It was eighteen months after the war ended, when my siblings and I were still pre-teens that my father fulfilled his dream of becoming self-employed. Using his savings as a down payment, he bought a fifteen-bedroom private hotel, on the coast of Somerset. On his insistence, while still responsible for the care of her growing family, Mother reluctantly took on the duties of hotel chef. When I enquired, (I might add, selfishly) why she needed to do the cooking—making her unavailable to her children for many hours a day—she told me, "My marriage vows were to obey my husband. This is my duty."

During our formative years, Mother did her best to instill a sense of duty and obedience in her four children, though I think we were all aware that it was not always with complete conviction.

She was utterly delighted and relieved to leave the hotel business, and often claimed, with a great deal of resentment, that she "lost" us all (her children) due to the long hours of work she felt duty-bound to do—affording her little time to attend to our upbringing.

The hotel in Somerset

◆   ◆   ◆

There was no hint of resentment in her voice, however, when on another of my noon calls, Mother told me in a tone of great pride and accomplishment, "All the clothes I will never wear again went to the charity shop. I've kept a few things, which my friends or Ann might like … after I've gone of course. And I've kept two of my favorite outfits—just in case I go anywhere special."

But she went nowhere special again. Not to the nearby race course, to stand in the sunshine admiring the brightly-colored silks of the jockeys straddling their mounts, or to thrill to the sight and sound of the gleaming, steaming thoroughbreds, thundering towards the winning post, a-blur against the backdrop of the fresh, green English countryside. Not even to the local pub for her favorite lunch of homemade soup and pâté. She was to go nowhere, ever again.

Stored drapes from prior homes, unused linens, small, less-favored, dust-gathering knick-knacks, duplicate kitchen items—everything she would no longer use or want to look at—were identified, labeled, and put away for disposal after her death. Favorite books, paintings, and cherished ornaments, delighted in for so many years, were marked discreetly with the name of each person designated to receive them, and left in their place. She was sorting everything out.

About three months after her surgery, I mailed Mother a slim book entitled, *Grandmother Remembers*. The book has lined, blank pages, with short, incomplete sentences printed at the top of each page intended to prompt memories to be written in by hand and, on a few pages, spaces are outlined for placement of photographs. I asked Mother if she had the energy and will to write brief accounts of her life in the book, and added, "If you do, will you give it to Anna (my daughter), this Christmas?" Mother gave her brave reply, "I can't promise that I'll complete it, but I'll give it my best shot."

Anna—and my two sons, Sándor and David—had lived in America since early childhood and, during a weeklong visit to her grandmother's home, just prior to Mother's last visit to our home in New Mexico, Anna developed a close bond with her.

Over the ensuing months, Mother completed each page of the book with thoughtful, brief, sentences, and favorite photos depicting her life from childhood to her eighties. She told me the book was difficult for her to complete "… because I so rarely think about myself, and you know what a private person I am." Today, this condensed, intimate autobiography is Anna's most treasured gift from her grandmother.

Sometimes, I felt concerned that some of my questions might intrude on my mother's natural reserve, but risked asking them anyway. During one phone call I asked her whether she had anything left unsaid to anyone that might be important for her to say, before she died, "… so that you can die feeling that your relationship with each person is complete." She said she would think about it. I intruded no further, knowing that if it was important to her she would get to it in her own time.

During another call, I asked her if she had chosen how she wanted her body dressed after her death. "Hmm! Now *that* hadn't occurred to me! Thank you for asking, dear. That will take some very careful consideration."

As always, Mother shied away from nothing, and a week later declared, "I've chosen it, dear." (She always called me dear.) "I've pinned a note to it. It says, 'This one, Judith!'"

I also asked her if she'd thought about the details of her funeral, and she replied, "No, I haven't done that yet. I'll save that conversation for when you come to take care of me. You know, at the end."

And the end was galloping headlong towards us.

◆   ◆   ◆

During Mother's months of organization and preparation, I often thought of my brothers and how they were dealing with the forecast of our mother's death. They also received a call from my sister about Mother's emergency hospitalization, and joined me at Mother's side. I was fortunate to spend some time with them during the days immediately following Mother's surgery, when we drove together in my rental car to visit Mother. On those hour-long journeys through the English country lanes, I joined in my brothers' conversations and gathered that providing care for the sick was definitely low on their list of preferences. Though, to give him credit, Kevin—during one of our stops for a meal at a road-side pub—generously offered, "If I lived closer, I would care for her. That is, if no one else is available."

Damian could make no such offer. He's the eldest child and an accomplished linguist. At that time he worked as a translator for a division of the United Nations, and lived with his love, TA, in a small, French village, just across the Swiss border. He has two sons—with his second wife—living in Geneva, and two older children living in England, with whom he has little contact. When we visited Mother in hospital Damian always dressed the same, in a comfortable track-suit, a cotton tee shirt, and flip flops—regardless of the weather.

Kevin, more comfortable in shirt, tie and two-piece suit, is the second child, and lives on the west coast of Spain, where he makes his living teaching English to lawyers, doctors, and other professionals. The income derived from his self-employment supports his passion for writing, and pursuing patents for his latest inventions. Always with a notebook in hand, it is quite usual to hear him chuckling to himself as he jots down his latest creative thought with his ever-ready pen or pencil; I observed him doing this several times when we were together at the hospital.

With the end of Mother's life forecast, would my brothers be able to take time from work to be with her, and perhaps help with her care?

And then there's, Ann, the third child, who enjoyed a successful career in the television industry and married in her early thirties. Prior to her marriage, however, she developed symptoms of agoraphobia, which increased in intensity over the next several years, to the extent that her husband left her, unwilling to live with a wife suffering from this insidious, yet outwardly indiscernible condition. Ann, a year or so after my father died, moved to the same village in which my mother lived and, despite living in dread of a panic attack, she checked on Mother's well-being daily, offering her what support she could. With her three siblings absent from the country, Ann felt a heavy burden of responsibility for Mother's well-being. It was when Ann joined me on a visit to see Mother in hospital—where she became faint and somewhat distraught at the sight of fluid-filled bottles with connecting tubes leading into Mother's body—that I realized she would be unable to offer Mother any more support than she was already giving. She had already given so much.

How would Mother's final weeks of care unfold?

◆   ◆   ◆

In May of the year following Mother's surgery, when I was attending a business conference in Santa Barbara, I called Mother at noon Greenwich Mean Time. After my greeting I heard, "Hello dear. I'm so glad you called; the doctor says it's time for you to come."

I felt my chest constrict like a deflating balloon as the breath rushed from my lungs. A numbing pain tightened around my eyes and my throat closed. I was aware of a sudden urgency to empty my bowels.

Then, as though talking about the weather, Mother continued calmly, "Are you still there, dear?"

Without waiting for my reply she continued, "Doctor came in today. He said I have about three weeks left and if I want you with me I'd better let you know right away. You will come dear, won't you?" Her tone was light, as though inviting me to a party.

Somehow surrendering to my fear, it dissolved, and I found my voice, "Yes, I'll come as soon as I can. I'll book a flight and call you back to let you know when I'm arriving."

As I heard my voice speaking I inhaled deeply, focusing on supporting her. This was not about *me*, not about *my* fear, not about *my* sadness. This was about my mother, *dying*. In three weeks? The twelve months forecast was now less than one.

Focusing on breathing calmly, I gathered my thoughts and senses, and opening my heart to her, I asked, "Are you afraid?"

"No dear, I'm not afraid. I'm waiting for *you*."

For the next twenty-four hours my preparations to leave proceeded apace: flights were booked; responsibilities at work transferred and, upon returning to our home in New Mexico, packing commenced for an indeterminate absence.

On the way to the airport, HB and I affirmed our intention to nurture ourselves, and one another, by talking regularly by phone and by corresponding, in writing, as often as possible.

I began writing to him two days later.

2

For the Duration

28th May
Friday 9:45 PM
Dusk

Hi dearest HB,

I arrived at Mother's late last night and am utterly jet-lagged. Mother wept as we whispered our hellos and held each other close.

"What a relief," she breathed into my ear, gulping down her tears. "I'm so glad you're here for the duration, dear. I'll be alright now!"

I remember how she had said that latter phrase when she was discharged from the hospital, where she was sent to convalesce after her surgery. Am I ready for this? There's no need for me to question; I'm here; I must be ready!

As I write, Mother is in bed—wearing a new lawn nightgown. She looks, and is, as beautiful as ever. Her physician has prescribed more medication. She takes twenty-three pills a day and six teaspoons of laxative and, she declared, that as of today, I am in charge of her medicines—then added, "It's all a bit too much for me to remember, now."

She tells me that tomorrow a friend is coming in to see her, and on Sunday, Sarah, my cousin, is stopping in, for what Mother hopes will be a short visit. She tires easily.

It reached 79°F today, with high humidity, and BBC television showed record crowds at the Royal Bath & West Show, with clips of the sports events for people with disabilities. This is the first year, for so many years, that you and I will not be attending the Show; I shall not go alone.

Mother needs my help going up and down stairs. Since my flying visit here a month ago, she seems more debilitated and weaker, though she's very peaceful and cheery.

Today, she shared a little about not knowing how to pray anymore, and wonders what comes after this—meaning life. After some thinking aloud she arrived at, "Perhaps *everything* is prayer when we speak silently to another." (I think she was referring to God.) It appears to concern her deeply, to be out of touch with her faith. If she brings the subject up again, I intend to encourage her to talk more about it.

Stay in touch please. I love you, kisses and hugs,
Ju

P.S. I intended to write my trip report of the Santa Barbara conference, and to read some of the documents that were handed out there; to no avail. Work seems so distant already, disconnected from this living and dying here.

◆   ◆   ◆

Just a few days prior to writing this first letter home, I was in Santa Barbara at a conference entitled "Diversity in U.S. Corporations." Attending conferences on this topic, whether as a participant or presenter, was a part of my job. For twenty-five years as a global diversity strategist for high tech corporations, I had held great passion for my work as a human resources consultant—it focused on improving productivity through specifically designed management practices to be applied in multicultural environments—and it involved much traveling, criss-crossing the United States; working in ten European countries; in Israel, and in Malaysia.

Now here I was in a small, ancient city, in Somerset County, in the southwest of England, where my father and dutiful mother finally chose to settle. To me, it felt more like a village than a city; I knew the place quite well, having visited annually since my parents moved there six years before my father died.

The narrow high street has a couple of greengrocers, two supermarkets, a butcher's shop, a newsagents, several charity shops, clothing and shoe shops, a dry cleaners, a bakery or two, a couple of book shops, and the typical English-city sprinkling of ancient pubs.

Each Saturday, an open market is set up in the cobbled market square at the top of the high street to which people from surrounding communities come in droves. Meandering around the stalls, they leaf through secondhand books, and thoughtfully finger their way through the racks of multi-colored cotton blouses, skirts, and gaudy shirts, all sporting stitched-in "Made in India" labels. Men and women alike, with wicker shopping baskets in hand, select judiciously from rows of neatly displayed, picked-this-morning produce, local cheeses, fresh fish, joints of beef, and even skinned rabbits hanging on hooks in the open air. The market is charged with the insistent energy of vendor's voices calling out their wares and prices, jiggling change in their apron pockets as their customers haggle for a good bargain.

As the years passed and Mother still enjoyed good health, she and Ann would occasionally join the bustling crowds at the market; after making purchases of fresh cut flowers and enjoying a companionable stroll around the stalls, they would stop at one of the ancient pubs to quaff a glass of wine, before heading off to their respective, and adjacent homes, just a quarter of a mile away.

This quaint venue was to be my place of residence for the duration of my mother's life.

3

Milestones

1st June

Dearest HB,

Mother is staying in bed again, today. She was in pain from when she awoke until about 10:00 AM, when the 8 AM dose of painkiller finally kicked in.

Her niece, Sarah, came to visit, and whispered in reverential tones, "How very hard this all is," and I wonder if we are on the same frequency. Death doesn't seem to be something to whisper about. But then, I need to remember that Mother and I have talked of *little else* for almost a year. It is what is. Sarah also indicated, out of Mother's hearing, "I'll be at the funeral, so will see you again soon."

After Sarah's visit, Mother and I lunched together in her bedroom. I sit in the armless chair—the one that converts into a single bed—with a tray on my lap, and Mother has her meal on a tray, which has legs that conveniently straddle her body.

I want to remind you of Mother's room, so you can picture us here. It is as full of character as the main Georgian house on which property it sits, but as it is the converted carriage house, her home has that lovely country cottage feel to it, with beamed ceilings and chintz drapes. When she moved in, Mother made the drapes by hand, adding a matching valance, bed and dressing-table skirt, and even the nightstand lampshade. The same, small ornaments are still on the deep window-sill: the two white, miniature, porcelain horses, and the Onyx sleeping fox, ears pricked, with tail curled around its muzzle. Behind these, there is a photo of Damian, taken at the top of the Sandia Tramway during his visit to us in New Mexico—his resemblance to Paul Newman as uncanny as ever.

On one of her three white bookcases, Mother has photos of all her brood, taken when we were toddlers. There's one of Damian, Kevin and Ann, beaming with delight, perhaps at some toy the photographer is holding high; this one and others are in miniature frames positioned near a photo of my father, very handsome at thirty-two, and some larger, more recent individual pictures of my siblings, and me. Hard to believe my father has been dead for twenty-one years; I find my mind wondering whether Mother thinks of him much these days.

The bookcases are filled with Dick Francis novels, and several books on English history by Winston Churchill, and well-worn, leather-bound books of poetry, including the Oxford Book of English Verse; when I was a child, I loved to sit in an overstuffed chair by the coal fire on a December night, and leaf through that book's flimsy, gilt-edged pages. I particularly loved to read Shakespeare's *Spring and Winter,* especially *Winter,* allowing the entire scene to unfold in my imagination.

The skylight, which Mother loves to have open whatever the weather, still has no blind or drape; she never wanted either. She told me this morning how she enjoys seeing the dawn sky blossoming into the day. In the early morning, she can hear the voices of her neighbors as they leave the converted stables across the way; she asked whether their voices disturb me. I hear them and they don't.

There is a TV in her room now, a fairly recent gift from Ann. As you well know, Ann has been Mother's companion and neighbor for nearly twenty years; many of her gifts are evident, as Mother points out, "... and that's another present from Ann."

The TV sits on a low table opposite the foot of Mother's bed and, when she is propped up with pillows, it is at just the right height for her to see the screen. The chair, where I sit to have my meals with her, faces her bed, which makes it easy to chat when we are munching our food—or when we just sit in view of one another, in companionable silence.

On the white, multi-drawer bureau, there's the small, ceramic bust of the Virgin Mary, her eyes closed, her hands clasped in prayer, (Mother has owned this since before any of her children were born). Next to the ceramic bust is her favorite photo of me. You may remember the one. I'm in a dusty-pink, cowl-necked sweater, taken before I wore specs. It is also here—on her bureau—where she likes to have vases of fresh flowers placed. There is always a full vase, visible from her bed, and the flowers' sweet scent pervades the room. Her favorite flower is the freesia. Heady! So different from her favored Chanel #5 perfume.

Soon after my arrival, Mother was quick to show me where she keeps the item of clothing in which she wants to be laid out. It is in the third drawer down of her bureau. My heart sank as she put it in my hands and I read the note pinned to it: "This one, Judith."

So these are the surroundings in which Mother has chosen to die. I remember her emphatic words on the phone, "I want to die in my own bed. *Promise* me you will *not* let me die in a hospital." And here we are, her death forecast, like the weather.

Vincent, the deacon from the local Catholic Church, came to give Mother Communion. He was full of supplication and small, bobbing, courteous bows, and said to me, as he left, "I am *so glad* you are here!" He says, next Sunday he'll bring the new priest, Father Jim, when Mother wants to arrange for the Last Rites.

Already, the closeness of the boundaries here has me selfishly raging with cabin fever. I feel so confined by the limits of the village, no matter how lovely it is. Perhaps I'll walk to one of the nearby hamlets for a pint of ale this evening, just to be in nature, and to feel the joy and freedom of space; there is none at the house, as in this illustration: if Mother hears me blow my nose, she calls out from her bed, in her concerned mother's voice, "You don't have a cold do you, dear?" If I'm quiet, or she sees me rest my eyes for a minute, she calls, "You don't have a migraine do you, dear?"

If I cough, I hear, "You don't have a cough do you, dear?"

I love her so and at the same time notice that her constant, dogging attention drives my mind to distraction. How selfish. I keep remembering to just surrender.

Damian called from France last night, and Mother relayed to me that he'd asked, "Do you think you're dying, Mother?"

It seems she'd replied. "Yes Damian, I do. I think I have two to three weeks left at the most."

"Oh God," was evidently his reply, and he went on to say he'd be here to see her in the next two weeks.

Kevin wrote to Mother from Spain. She gave his letter to me to read, a sweet, comforting, supportive communication.

Ann stated that she has "… resigned completely." This was said in the context of me "… having taken over *everything*."

After being Mother's constant and only family support since our father's death, I think she's more than willing to surrender the heavy responsibility she has borne for so long. Though petite in build and stature, Ann's shown such strength and constancy during Mother's illness, but this is somewhat belied now, by the ever-present expression of anxiety in her china-blue eyes. She hasn't come in yet today; perhaps she will later.

·Gwen, the district nurse, who, Mother says with dread, "… is trained to give enemas," is supposed to come today, though at 1:30 there's no sign of her yet. There are several different health care resources who attend Mother. There is Wendy, an LPN, and according to Mother, either Gwen or Wendy visit once a week, to check on Mother's care needs, and then there is someone called Cindy. And, of course, the indispensable caregivers, Hazel and Rachel, who visit every Monday, Wednesday and Friday. Soon I will need them to come every day, as bathing Mother safely is difficult for the untrained.

Last night, after you called—and while Mother took her evening calls from her sister, Norah, then Damian, then Kevin—I took your advice, and strolled round to the City Arms Pub, and sat at one of the tables in the cobbled courtyard, nursing a pint of ale for an hour. I've asked Mother's callers to phone in the evening, after Mother's retired to her bed for the night. She much prefers to avoid the former, all-too-frequent hassle of having to hang on to the furniture as she maneuvered herself across the sitting room to reach the phone; it is so misplaced at the bottom of the stairs in the hallway. It's agonizing to observe how weak Mother's become. She won't hear of a cordless phone, "Hardly at this late stage, dear."

A Touch of Frost (one of the BBC mysteries), was on TV last night, it was a two-hour show. Mother and I watched it in her room. I'd seen it before and enjoyed it again—it brought you closer somehow; something we've shared.

Today, there are white puffy clouds, a crystal blue sky, and a light breeze, and jackdaws are chatting on the tiled roofs of the converted stables across the way.

I'm reading *Stieglitz and O'Keeffe*. There are many ways I identify with O'Keeffe's love of open spaces and barren landscapes. It's the freedom my spirit feels, without containment, when horizons are so distant.

I miss your presence, our togetherness, and the peace of our Sanctuary. But I'm here, where I want to be, to fulfill my promise to Mother, to support her during her dying process, including being her "rock" (as she is calling me still). I want her to rely on me in any way she needs to, emotionally, mentally, physically, and even spiritually. I want this time with her to somehow fill out the fifty-one-week physical gaps in our relationship for the past too-many years—not that she would ever see it that way. My long absences from her—until you and I lived in Switzerland anyway—deprived us of each other's physical presence, and ways to regularly express, in person, the love that has always been present between us. How fortunate I am to have this opportunity to demonstrate it to her now. My heart is filled with her.

Send me a Polaroid or two of the courtyard and gardens, would you? Any; just so I can be in that space with you.

I love you,
Ju

◆   ◆   ◆

The artistic talent that my mother brought to the interior décor of her bedroom was present in many other areas of her life. Having been denied the completion of her art school education, she expressed her dreams of contributing to the world of haute couture by making stylish clothes for herself, and her two daughters. Her aestheticism was also revealed in her sketches, oil paintings, embroidery, and classic knits. And in her thirties and forties, when she and my father attended local society balls, she would always wear a stunning, full-length gown that she had designed and made herself; when I was a child my father loved to tell (and I loved to hear) how Mother was always the center of attention as he whirled her about the dance floor; as light as pixie dust on her feet and the epitome of grace in every movement. Everything Mother touched was infused with a heightened sense of form, beauty, and elegance.

Decades before, several years after I emigrated from London to Massachusetts with my first husband, and three small children, I began returning to England annually to visit my parents and sister in the West Country. My first husband and children accompanied me only once, the air fares for a family of five precluding that pleasure on a more regular basis. How fortunate that they joined me that once; it was the last time my children saw their grandfather. He died a year later on an April night, hours before I was to fly in for my annual week's visit, and to celebrate my parent's forty-third wedding anniversary.

After my first husband and I divorced, my career opened up with opportunities for relocation and travel, and eventually, for international assignments. When I moved from Massachusetts to Arizona, I gave Anna, my daughter—who opted to join me when I left my marriage—a choice to come and live with me in Arizona, or stay near her brothers. The latter had elected to stay with their father. Anna was seventeen then, and a senior in high school. Not wanting to make a choice at all, she angrily chose to stay with friends, and then went on to college in New England.

After two years in Arizona, on one of my frequent travels to the east coast for meetings, Anna invited me to spend a long weekend with her. It was then that she chose to confront me with her deep feelings of abandonment. Her confrontation transformed our relationship, for which I am forever grateful; her courage, her ability to understand her emotional pain, learn from it, accept it, and move on, continues to inspire me. Since then, she and I have enjoyed total acceptance of one another, and a deep and abiding friendship. She is a wise and beautiful woman.

I also recall feeling deep gratitude, when my eldest son, Sándor, after going to college in Massachusetts, and David, my youngest, after his high school graduation, came to live with me in Arizona. Sándor came to find work, which he soon did, and David to attend college.

It occurs to me that some souls bond for a time (children with their parents are just one example), then spin away from one another to unfold a new chapter of their life on earth; perhaps to not meet again; perhaps to reunite, to complete the relationship in person.

HB and I first met in New England, our professional lives crossing at the same corporation. We met again in Arizona, six years later. A loving friendship developed over several years, during which time his wife, from whom he was separated, died of cancer. He and I married a year after her death. It was shortly after our wedding that HB was diagnosed with malignant melanoma.

His recovery from surgery coincided with my taking a six-month assignment in England, where, as he was now retired, he accompanied me. By this time, Mother was diagnosed with chronic leukemia and her health was declining to the extent that she doubted that she would survive the winter, due to recurring bronchitis and pneumonia. Over that winter and spring, HB and I spent as many days with Mother and Ann as my travel schedule allowed. It was a special time for us all. HB healed, and Mother's health rallied, which she attributed partly to our frequent visits, saying, as we left to return to the United States, "Thank you for spending so much time with me, your visits have been spiritually renewing."

In spring of the following year, I was reassigned to the company's headquarters in Geneva for a couple of years, and HB also accompanied me there. We made frequent weekend trips to see Ann and Mother, and in late May, HB and I started a tradition of going to the Royal Bath and West Show: a very large agricultural fair, held annually for over three hundred consecutive years.

One May, though still suffering from many exhausting symptoms, Mother accompanied us to the show. She loved the warm, spring sunshine. We took a picnic and spread a blanket on the newly mown grass, and munched on fresh fruit and local cheeses. HB uncorked a bottle of chilled wine, and we saluted one another's health, quietly sharing details of what had caught our attention at the show. The sheep-shearing demonstration, equestrian competitions, and the vast flower tent were Mother's and my favorites. Mother was especially taken by the delphiniums, in all their glorious shades of blue. HB was more attentive to the latest farm equipment on display, the livestock shows, the leather crafts, and country-food vendors.

During these frequent weekend visits, HB and Mother developed a light-hearted relationship, their similar sense of humor and the pleasure they took in one another's company, always evident. When they walked together anywhere, at the Royal Bath & West Show, or when strolling to a village pub for a glass of wine, Mother always linked her arm in his and, as they chatted about this and that, she would look up at him, smiling, listening intently to what he had to say.

While I was with Mother during her last weeks, HB wrote to her every day. She loved receiving his letters and expressed deep gratitude for his thoughtfulness.

◆   ◆   ◆

2nd June

Dearest HB,

It's Monday. Hazel came in to bathe Mother and change her linen; I went to the High Street to shop for fresh vegetables, fish, and chicken. The greengrocer and the butcher asked after Mother; I find their concern touching.

Earlier this morning I cleaned the kitchen cupboards inside and out, and swabbed the two rubbish bins, which sit out on the patio. The latter were odorous, to say the least. Not a task Mother could have managed in recent years and one she would not ask Ann to do.

I was aware of much hot anger rising this morning—as it seems to do, both irrationally and regularly, at the most trivial things—like the kettle taking too long to boil for tea! I noticed a tight feeling in my chest, my head pounding, and my jaw clenching. I keep reminding myself that anger is one of the natural stages of grief, and remembering makes it easier to accept, allowing it to dissolve, and I become present again.

Anna wrote the loveliest good-bye to Mother. How wise my daughter is, so open and loving.

She also wrote an encouraging note to me, reminding me to be at peace with what is, and to stay present. Staying in the present does bring inner stillness and peace. It is when my mind leaps out into the future that presence escapes me, and my body fills with tension, and fear invades my mind and emotions. I welcomed Anna's reminder.

Mother seemed deeply touched by Anna's letter to her, though she remained completely dry-eyed. Later, she handed it to me to read, and I read it in 'my' room behind closed doors and let the tears flow—consciously allowing my grief to emerge. I notice how easy it would be, to become self-indulgent with grief.

I'm catching up on overdue letters, to friends, and my aunts, and cousins, who sent the genealogy information that I'd requested of them. Perhaps you remember? It arrived just before I left? The expansion of the family tree awaits future attention.

My friend, Diane, writes that she's just graduated with a certificate in Landscape Architecture and Design. As you know, she and I share a passion for gardens, though we have different design preferences, as you and I do—yours is classic; structured; neat and tidy; while mine is unstructured, bursting with color, and wild abandon.

I'm writing to David and Sándor today, to convey to them how important it is to me that they join Anna at our Sanctuary for the July 4th weekend. Mother frets that I might miss the long-planned reunion. I do want all my children to be there together, with you, whether I am there or not.

Rachel has gone to London with her husband, to keep an appointment with her gynecologist. Hazel has accompanied them as additional support. Rachel is making another in utero fertilization attempt, and is naturally anxious. Mother tells me it is the final attempt (of many) and worries on Rachel's behalf. It will be some weeks before Rachel knows whether the procedure has been successful.

As always, Mother sends her love to you along with mine,
Ju

P.S. It has clouded over, and there is an east wind, though it's still bright and pleasant.

◆   ◆   ◆

With my daughter Anna's permission, her last letter to her grandmother reads:

"Dear Gran,

You've been in my thoughts and heart constantly. I'm hoping you're staying comfortable. I'm sending you a constant flow of warm, comfy love, and hope it reaches you, and you snuggle up, allowing it to envelope you with comfort, peace, and clarity.

I've just looked through my "Grandmother Remembers" book again, and am so deeply grateful to you for putting it together for me. You've always been in my thoughts and my heart, and now I even have you in my hands.

I'm so glad you are allowing Mom to support you in all the ways you want. I can't think of anyone I'd rather spend such an important time with. Such incredible trust and love, to know she is there for you one hundred percent. She is so amazing, I adore her, too. It must be incredibly satisfying to see your child develop, as an extension of you, into such an amazing woman. What a legacy to leave. If there are times when your body's discomfort distracts you from the peace and abundance of love that surrounds you, focus on your daughter.

I'm fully aware that you both have taught me so much about being a woman. We make a difference, and touch lives, by just being who we are.

Gran, you *will* be remembered by those of us who are a part of you. I love you and cherish who you are, and all that I've become because of you, and the life you've lived. And as I touch the world, continuing to focus, and touch the world some more, I'll think of you while doing so. You are with me, forever.

I love and cherish you, Gran.

Love,
Anna

◆   ◆   ◆

When HB's estranged wife was diagnosed with cancer, I thought it beneficial to learn about the stages of grief. It was important to me that I understand what he, and his sons and daughter, might be going through. To this end I read several books, mostly by Elisabeth Kubler-Ross, on the subject of loss and grief. She was the accepted expert on the subject at the time. Her writing helped me to understand HB's roller-coasting emotions throughout the period of his wife's illness and their separation, and allowed me to support him more fully. The stages of grief include: denial; anger; bargaining; depression, and acceptance.

While caring for Mother, I was unaware of any depression or bargaining. However, I was conscious of occasional feelings of denial, and quite frequent internal explosions of anger. Becoming aware of my denial and anger, as part of the natural grieving process, allowed me to relinquish them and, in so doing, the emotion would dissolve, and I could dwell in stillness and acceptance, again.

Mother lived almost every moment with acceptance, voicing resistance to her death on only one or two occasions.

A year earlier, Anna—who lived in Florida at the time with her partner, John, and their eight year old son, Jordan—suggested that over the following July 4th weekend, she and her brothers, together with their loved ones, reunite at the Sanctuary. My children had not spent time together—or together with me—for many years, and a reunion was something she and I longed for. We wanted an opportunity to be in one another's presence at the same time, and to hear about one another's lives, and strengthen bonds with each other, and with new family members.

Based on some personal history, of what Anna referred to then, as "brotherly neglect," she doubted that her older brother, Sándor, would show up for the reunion. Sándor lived in California and was deeply engrossed in a new career. He seemed to focus solely on work, rarely communicating with his sister or brother, and on only rare occasions, initiating phone calls to me. Anna was deeply saddened by the absence of Sándor in her life, and that of her family. David, my youngest, lived in Phoenix, with his wife, Susan; they were expecting their first child. David was eager for the reunion, and Sándor expressed some interest in it as well.

When, during the ensuing months, Anna and I spoke occasionally with Sándor about the arrangements for the reunion, we colluded with what we both heard as a lack of commitment in his voice. Now, I look back and think how foolish that was of us! The law of attraction always gives us what we focus on, and we focused on him not showing up! Nonetheless, in my ignorance at the time, I expected him to be there.

HB knew my children well. They came to our wedding, welcoming him into my life as a dear friend, husband, and lover. HB was also looking forward to the gathering at the Sanctuary.

◆   ◆   ◆

3rd June

Dear HB,

Two letters came from you this morning. What a horrific turn of events to get an urgent call from your sister, Eleanor, about Lucie's fall, and to hear Lucie's subsequent decision to "… go to bed and die." I deeply empathize and understand that you cannot bring yourself to visit your mother as she lies dying. Everyone deals with death differently. Wanting to remember Lucie the way we saw her in April is *your* way of dealing with it.

I can visualize her now, as she dined with us at the Jail House Restaurant; chuckling quietly at something you said; then later, in her garden, pointing with her gnarly, arthritic fingers, with such voiced pleasure, at the upturned faces of the purple and yellow pansies against the dark, rich, Cape Cod earth. Your sisters wanting to be there with her, is *their* way of dealing with it. Witnessing my mother dying is heartrending, yet I wouldn't miss this time with her. That's *my* way. Allow your grief to flow as it emerges. Suppressing it will only lead to ill-health, later.

I lay awake in the early hours of this morning listening for sounds of Mother stirring, and couldn't hear any. I breathed in peace and calm, trying to remember the first calls I'd need to make—doctor, siblings—but it was just my mind, creating a false alarm.

She is weaker today, though very peaceful, and in no pain. She couldn't rise from a supine to sitting position without my help, and was very shaky as we went shuffling along to the bathroom, even with my arm firmly about her. She thinks she won't go downstairs again, and that's probably wise, from the perspective of my ability to lift and carry her—for any distance.

Earlier, Mother asked me if I'd ever commit suicide; after some thought, I replied, "Not because of some perceived sadness. But if I was terminally ill, I would probably consider it."

"Yes," she said, "I might deal with it that way, too."

If she does, I know I will not help her. And she would never ask me.

She's been reading a book I gave her, called *Final Gifts*. It's an account by two Hospice nurses of their work with terminally-ill patients. Mother says she finds it, "… lovely to dip into! There are so many ways to die."

From when Mother wakes, it takes up to three hours to complete her breakfast and mine, to wash her face and hands, brush her hair, and to administer her medications; then the bed-making, dish washing, laundry, bathing myself, and generally cleaning up around the house. By 10:00 AM, which it is now, she usually sleeps for a while, and I take some time to be with you.

Mother conveys in many ways how much she wants and even needs me here—for quiet, peaceful company, and emotional support, as well as for attention to her physical needs, except for the full-body bathing. Either Hazel, or Rachel, comes in every other day to do that for which I am deeply grateful. I'm happy to provide everything I can for Mother. It is the greatest privilege to be included in the intimacy of her conscious living-with-dying process.

Mother asked me to patch the worn armrest of her favorite armchair, and the lining of her bedroom drapes; the latter disintegrated when they were laundered earlier in the spring. These items are two of very few things on her list that she didn't get to. She has always been such a role model for one of our family scripts, "If it needs doing, do it now, or know when it will get done." However, as sewing is something for which I have no finesse, it is a non-starter on my list; I gently declined her request and she acceded.

It looks like rain today. It is much cooler. The house is so quiet and peaceful.

After talking with you last evening, I went to the City Arms for a pint and to sit in the flower-festooned courtyard; all other patrons were inside. The night air was quite cool, and the tranquility and space were welcome gifts. The courtyard has an umbrella plant, similar to the one in our lily pond.

HB, I cannot fathom that before you get this letter, Mother may have left; and Lucie! It is so hard for my heart and mind to accept. Denial comes so swiftly. What a challenging time. So be it.

As it's close to Mother's morning coffee time, I'll end here, with love, hugs, and kisses.

I love you, HB.
Ju

◆   ◆   ◆

4th June
Morning

Hi Love,

Today, Mother is having a better day. She asked me to shampoo her hair again, as Kevin arrives tomorrow, and she wants to look her best; she says she feels so well that she feels guilty about me being here.

As Hazel and Rachel are away, Wendy is due to come in to take care of the full-body ablutions. While she's here I'll go and catch the post and do some grocery shopping.

Last night, after I'd given Mother her 8:00 PM medications, Ann and I enjoyed supper together at the City Arms. Ann is dreading and, at the same time, yearning for this to end. Yearning, she says, for when, "… we can all be put out of our misery," and dreading, because of her anticipated loneliness. I empathize deeply with her feelings, as there are no other family members within hailing distance of her.

Thanks for your lovely letters, they fill me with you. Will you mail me some packets of Good Earth tea, please? Just drinking a favorite tea helps me feel connected to you, to have something I'm used to that we enjoy together.

I wrote to Lucie this morning, and hope it reaches her before she dies.

I love you,
Ju

Same day
In the PM

Hi Sweetheart,

Christine, the podiatrist, is upstairs attending to Mother. Christine has been coming to take care of Mother's feet (and sometimes even her hands) for a year or two. They have become friends, and are enjoying a chat, and a cup of tea.

This morning Mother said, in an unequivocal tone, "Judith, I've decided that I shall stay in bed now, until I die. I just don't have the strength to oppose gravity anymore, and cannot haul my body upstairs again, even with your help." She went on to add, "Going downstairs isn't so bad, but it's too risky, as I don't think I can climb them again." Then, raising her eyebrows, she asked, with great concern, "Do you mind, dear?"

"Not at all, Mother, I support whatever you want to do."

So be it—a major milestone reached and it seemed to give her no difficulty at all. Her grace and acceptance amaze me.

While Wendy bathed her, I decided to tackle a milestone of my own and went to the undertakers to pre-arrange Mother's funeral. The entire time I was there, I consciously focused on my breathing, knowing that I was apt to burst into tears at the slightest provocation of my mind.

I was led quietly into a room, carpeted, glassed, and heavily curtained, with low lighting, and a well-placed box of Kleenex on the desk. The woman, Shirley H___, sat across from me, a framed certificate above her head, which read:

Shirley H ____,

PASSED

Interpersonal Skills, Funeral Arrangements,
Professional and Personal Needs of the Family
Funeral Products and Services

Signed ...   Dated ...

Shirley was both kind and businesslike, and I distanced myself emotionally from the proceedings by wondering if she was top of her class. The funeral, all inclusive, will cost a little more than £1500. I followed Mother's verbal instructions to the letter, and arranged for the following:

1.   The cheapest coffin possible

2.   No frills of any sort

3.   No flowers *at all*—except from her children

4.   Cremation

5.   A plaque to be placed *next to* my father's, in the Garden of Remembrance

Mother further clarified "next to," by adding "not above and not below." So that's what is arranged.

I noticed my ego *wanting* Mother to have the best that could be afforded, yet she wouldn't entertain any of my suggestions. Next, I have to see the new priest to work out the arrangements for the Requiem Mass. We (the kids) must take care of ordering our wreath from the florist on the corner of Priest Row, and getting it delivered to the mortuary the night before the funeral.

Ann has alerted the executor of Mother's Will. He was "most sad" to hear of Mother's condition.

Damian seems (to me) to be nonplussed about what action to take. He called me this morning to ask, "How is Mother really? I can't afford to keep coming and going." (Child-support payments are still a financial burden, and he probably has limited vacation time.) I told him I'd talk to Mother about his comment, and ask her what she wants. So having done that, when Damian calls tonight, she will tell him that I will let him know two to three days in advance (!) and otherwise, to come just for the funeral. I think he'll be content with that, and so is Mother.

Edna, ninety years of age—a neighbor, who lives at #8 in the Georgian house to which Mother's home is attached—stopped by the front gate to say hello, and ask after Mother. She was matter-of-fact about my comments, nodding her head and saying "Yes, well …" She was quite unsentimental. Perhaps it will come to us all in time, complete acceptance of what is, in *every* moment. Such stillness and peace accompanies presence.

Wendy commented that Mother may continue the way she is for weeks, and added that we should expect a hepatic coma, "When the odor gets really bad, and there's any sign of jaundice that will be a signal."

I'm glad to have some people here who aren't into the drama of death and tell it the way it is. No gloss.

It's so obvious that despite her mental alertness, Mother is declining each day. I shampooed her hair this morning, her head hanging over the basin in the bathroom. She was very shaky. I don't know if she'll be able to tolerate it that way again.

I sent a very pretty pansy card to Lucie this morning. I hope it reaches her in time. That each of us is losing our mother at the same time is very hard to take in. It is such an individual experience. No one can do it for us. How fortunate we are, to be able to support one another, even though we are six thousand miles apart. Thanks sweetheart, for your constant, loving support, by phone and letters.

Despite a forecast of thunder and rain showers spreading from Spain to the British Isles, it is a particularly beautiful day: clear blue skies, light breeze, warming sun, about 68°F.

For lunch, we're having garlic-buttered turkey breast, new potatoes slathered in butter, peas, and stewed apples for dessert. I don't know where all the food is going, as despite her adamant assurance that, "I *went* on Monday evening," Mother hasn't evacuated her bowels since last Wednesday. She is hoping to avoid an enema tomorrow. I wonder if constipation matters at this point.

I'm missing having my hands in the earth at our Sanctuary, and am sublimating by taking care of Mother's patio plants, where the work I did during my flying visits here in February and April, has borne fruit—well, it has borne flowers, actually! The pots get watered daily, and everything is now ablaze with reds, yellows, and subtle shades of green. Each flowering plant and miniature shrub is thriving, and as I potter about I can disappear for a while, into the stillness of nature.

Earlier, Mother thanked me for the plant care and, as an afterthought, she said, very softly, to herself, "I'm so sorry I won't see my patio flowers again." My tears oozed out.

Ann is coming round this evening, to do her laundry. I may go out for a break while she's here. No more news. Many hugs, and soft kisses,

Be well, we'll talk soon,
Ju

◆   ◆   ◆

5th June
Morning

Hi dear HB,

As usual I was up at 7:00—awake since 5:00. I'm over jet lag, and my body is finally on the local time zone.

Mother still likes to do her own ablutions when she feels up to it, and after breakfast, when I helped her to the bathroom, my lack of alertness, combined with her wobbly state, caused us to almost trip over each other's feet. To avoid a spill I must exercise great care, and remain completely present in every moment.

Between approximately 7:00 and 10:00, the activity here is the same every morning. It includes washing Mother's face and hands with a warm, well-squeezed-out, natural sponge; administering her medications, and assisting her on and off the commode, which the district nurse delivered yesterday. (If Mother doesn't have the energy, this new resource saves her shuffling to the bathroom, though she much prefers to use the bathroom when she can.) Other tasks include emptying and disinfecting the commode, and preparing, and taking up breakfast. If Mother perches on the commode long enough, and before the arrival of Hazel or Rachel, I also change her bed. Then it's time to do the laundry, wash the dishes, clean the house, and water the patio pots (even if it looks like rain). There is plenty to maintain. This morning I changed my bed linen also, and hung the first lot of washing, (you may remember that Mother has no dryer!) and the second load of washing is in. Since then, I've made coffee for Mother and tea for me, and it is now 10:20 AM.

No substitute has come to replace Rachel. Perhaps no one else will come while she and Hazel are away. Even Wendy has gone on vacation now.

This afternoon, when the weekly R.N. comes in, I'll have a word about Mother needing a caregiver to bathe her every day of the week. I can wash Mother's back, front and limbs, and on her short trips to the bathroom, Mother has been washing her face and "down under" (as she and her caregivers refer to genitals). But to ensure that she's completely clean, and that creams get applied to avoid bed sores, I know it's better for the professional caregivers to do the full-body bathe.

Mother looks very pretty today; as when you saw her last, her baby-fine hair is still almost completely ash-blonde, just a few silvery hairs blended in around her temples, and as a result of the medications all her age-lines have smoothed out.

She becomes such a dazzling bon vivant in front of any visitors that Kevin will wonder why he came. That is, until he sees her trying to walk and sees her abdomen, so swollen with the malignancy. Mother has tried to hide the latter by wearing loose-fitting tops, a design she never wore before this past year. The medications are also causing blotches of darker pigmentation on her arms, and legs. They look like small burns, dark reddish-brown.

Last night, Mother told Damian not to come before the funeral. She said to him, "We have many happy memories, don't we, dear? So there's really no need."

Damian told her he's arranged to come for a visit anyway, on the 27th, so unless she dies before, that's when he's coming. Kevin arrives today.

Thanks for two more letters; that's four in eight days, which I appreciate and horde.

I love you, and send kisses and hugs, and a pat for Ollie,
Ju

Same day
10:45 PM

Dear HB,

I want to get this content written before I forget it. After Ann and I got back from the City Arms, I sat with Mother for a while and brought up a conversation she'd begun earlier in the day, about her values. I asked her if she'd like to clarify her primary value, which this morning she said she didn't know. "Yes, I would," she declared.

So I wrote out a list of thirty values—all that I recall from the public workshops we used to conduct around the United States and Europe; the list of thirty defined itself appropriately. Then I asked her to select twelve of the thirty, which she did, slowly, and with much thought. The next step was for her to select five of the twelve.

With a concentrated frown, and her tongue held thoughtfully between her teeth, she selected, and deselected. This took her half an hour. On five strips of paper I wrote down her final five—one on each strip—then informed her, "Your task now is to select one of the five and surrender it to me," and so on, one at a time, until the final two. The first she gave up was Physical Health and Well-being; the second, Development of Ability; the third, Faith; the fourth, Family Happiness.

"All these are the same to me really," she kept murmuring.

As she hesitatingly passed me her fourth choice, she clutched the fifth to her breast—Home and Family. Quite overcome, she caught her breath, deeply moved. Then, reaching for my hand she pulled me to her, saying, "Thank you for doing this darling. I should have known all along. This *is* what I've always held as more valuable than anything else." Her face, now radiating happiness, she whispered, "And now, you have all come home to be with me." And she lay there, silent, smiling, her eyes closed, tears spilling, holding my hand. And I pictured us all here: Ann, a constant; Kevin, due in from Spain any moment, and Damian arriving from France on the 27th.

I asked Mother then, if she felt complete with all of us, if there was anything left unsaid that she needed or wanted to say, in order to feel at peace with each one of us.

She thought about this for a few minutes, while I sat in silence. "I think I still have something I need to say to Ann. I've tried before … but I don't know what else to say."

I ventured quietly, "If you put yourself in her place, what would you want to hear?"

She fell silent, slowly smoothing the coverlet over her abdomen, as though the movement helped her to shape her thoughts. Then she whispered, "I think if I was Ann I'd want to know that I was loved *more* than anyone else." Then she looked up at me and said, "Yet I *can't* tell her that because it's not true. I love you all the *same*."

"Then, what is true?" I asked.

"What's true is that I've always loved her. She's had so much pain in her life. That's why it is difficult for us sometimes. We seem to get at cross-purposes."

Not needing any explanation, I prompted, "Then you've felt some difficulty communicating what you want to say to her?"

"Exactly!"

"Could you tell her that?"

With a toss of her head, she cried, "Then she'd think she'd pulled one over on me."

This gave me momentary pause, and I conjectured, "Is there a bit of an ego struggle going on between you?"

She looked at me, her eyes widening with self-realization, "You've hit the nail on the head. Yes, I'm afraid there is. My ego *is* in my way. Oh, how dreadful. I'm so ashamed."

Contemplating, she returned to smoothing the coverlet again, her eyes following the movement of her hands as they brailed across her swollen abdomen. Not wanting to intrude further, we spoke no more of it, and I began to prepare her for bed.

She shuffled slowly to the bathroom, leaning heavily into me as I supported her around her bony shoulders. She cleaned her teeth, laboriously, gave herself a quick "lick and a promise," (as she'd always called the impatient ablutions of her rushing-to-play children), and shuffled back to bed, where I tucked her in with a gentle hug and kissed her goodnight. Then I collapsed on to my bed to await Kevin's arrival. He arrived ten minutes later. But that's for another letter.

I love you, kisses,
Ju

◆   ◆   ◆

At the age of twenty-three, (when my sister, Ann, was little more than a year old), my mother hemorrhaged severely during a miscarriage, which was followed by a year of debilitated health. I was born when my sister was just two and a half years old.

With my father away working from Monday to Friday, Mother felt perpetually tired from caring for four children, all under the age of five. Her health weakened further, and she and my father made what can only have been a monumentally difficult and heartrending decision. They decided to send Ann, not yet four, to board at a local convent, where nuns took care of her for many, many months. My brothers went to a local infant school each weekday morning, and with Ann in—what my parents considered—good hands, Mother was able to get some rest and care for me.

Mother always seemed reluctant to answer questions about the time Ann was boarded at the convent, "It seemed to be the only option at the time," was the most she would say, always looking aggrieved whenever the subject was broached. The event was an ever-present sore in their relationship, and I can only imagine what deep pain lay behind it for them both—so deep, it seemed inexpressible.

The time away from the family at such an early age had a deep and lasting impact on Ann. She lost all sense of family security and this feeling remained with her throughout her youth, and followed her into adulthood. The impact of her "banishment," as she referred to it, was underestimated by our parents, and certainly not understood then by any us, her siblings.

In her mid-twenties, Ann began to suffer from symptoms of agoraphobia, which worsened in her thirties to the extent that she abandoned her career, and eventually sought professional help. Today, she manages her life completely effectively, despite a persistent undercurrent of anxiety.

The pain that engulfed Ann's life—to which Mother referred—was compounded by Damian moving to Europe; my family and I immigrating to the

United States; the sudden death of our father, and abandonment by her husband—all over a span of twelve years.

◆   ◆   ◆

6th June

Dearest HB,

Now that Kevin is here—another body in the house—I'm feeling even more confined and sorry for myself, again! There is no space for privacy to replenish my energy, except in 'my' little bedroom, which has a single bed, nightstand, the wardrobe, and the laundry stand. So to say it is a bit cramped … but better than sleeping on the sofa—which Kevin is doing.

He arrived at 10:00 last night, his round face, pale, and his usually straight brow somewhat furrowed. Otherwise, he's looking well, and much the same—light blue, smiling eyes; his full lips now crowned with a trim moustache; however, the grayness of his hair surprised me.

He bounced upstairs to Mother's room, to say hello and goodnight, then came down to share his most recently registered patents, and his, thus far, unsuccessful attempts to sell his books on the Internet. As always, however, he remains optimistic.

After breakfast this morning, Kevin talked with Mother for an hour, when she called for me to take her to the bathroom. Her legs are even weaker today, and she leans right into me with her arm around my waist as I support her, with my arm hooked under her armpit. Her body is pitifully thin. It takes us a full two minutes to shuffle from her bed to the bathroom, and the same to get back. It can't be more than twenty-five feet—one-way.

She slept again, until Rachel arrived, the latter bringing with her a wonderfully fresh, beautiful bunch of huge red poppies and sweet-smelling roses, from her own garden; droplets of morning dew on the petals catching the light, reflecting the skylight in Mother's room.

What a lovely young woman Rachel is, full of positive energy and life. She has the deepest brown-velvet eyes and thick, shoulder-length, glossy brown hair. She is compassion personified. She has finished bathing Mother, and they're chatting now, over a cup of tea. I can hear Rachel telling Mother how long she has to wait, before she knows whether the medical procedure was successful.

Yesterday, I attempted a first draft of Mother's obituary. Ann has added to it, and I'll ask Kevin to do so, today. The date of death will be the only thing missing. I need to go to the undertakers with Mother's explicit instructions for the wording on the plaque, to be placed *next* to my father's.

This afternoon I'm going to the village and will call you while I'm out, as there's no way to make or take a private call, now that Kevin's here.

I do hope Lucie is comfortable. How wonderful that each of your three children called her to say good-bye.

Love, please take care of your aching back. Based on your letters, I think you have done too much yard work. Hopefully, by now, you've been to see the chiropractor. With the flight to Cape Cod looming, your back needs to be in the best possible shape.

I love you sweetheart, kisses and hugs,
Ju

◆   ◆   ◆

7th June
9:15 AM

Dearest HB,

Mother is in the bathroom cleaning her teeth and washing her face and hands. This takes about fifteen minutes, as she has to use one hand to balance herself, holding on to the washbasin all the while; she insists on doing it alone, and says emphatically, "I shall do it for as long as I can."

These short excursions to the bathroom are good for her circulation and, hopefully, will stay any development of bed sores. She has none, as yet.

Today is Derby day. The horse I picked for you is named, Single Empire, at odds of 33–1. I thought the name reminiscent of the Sanctuary. To celebrate three of Mother's children being here with her, and as a pre-Derby tailgate party—how *very* American that sounds!—we're having a family picnic in Mother's bedroom. This was Kevin's splendid idea, and Mother is delighted.

We are planning the inevitable family-picnic-fare: smoked, Scottish wild salmon with lemon wedges; asparagus tips; brown bread and butter; steaming new potatoes slathered in butter, and champagne—with an extra flute for the doctor, in case he pops in while we're eating; not that I think he'll join us in a glass.

While Kevin stayed in, Ann and I went to the City Arms again last night, it's good for us both to take a break to spend some time together. The conversation rarely veers from the situation at hand.

Two letters came from you today. I appreciate you writing so often, your letters are treasures that keep us connected to each other's day-to-day.

Kevin has gone to pick up a couple of things from the shops. I watched him leave, his head inclined to one side, his stride, long and rolling, as always. While he's out I shall write to Damian, to keep him up to speed on all the arrangements we're making.

Mother is sleeping now, and I have some rare space; I'm off to bathe, and then to post this to you, my love. (I sure do miss our shower.)

Kisses, and long, close hugs,
Ju

P.S. I've devised a new way to lighten up Mother's daunting excursions to the bathroom. They are so arduous for her, and she becomes very quiet as we trek our way there. Now, with me on her right, with my left arm supporting her, and her cane in her left hand, with her right arm about my waist, we have begun to dance our way there to the signature tune of the great Joe Loss band, *In the Mood*. For variety, I also throw in my rendition of *Little Brown Jug,* for the return journey. As we dance to and from the bathroom, Mother makes little bobs, and her steps get lighter as I swing us very carefully around, scatting "Doo-ba-da-ba-daa-ba-da-ba-daa-ba-da-da," that glorious big band music from the '40s and '50s, to which Mother loved to dance so long ago. I can actually feel her mood lighten and, as we pass the mirror on the landing, she takes a quick peek at her feet, stepping around mine, and chuckling she looks up at me, beaming, and gently squeezes me with her right arm. She is such a sweet, lovely, courageous woman. She *never* complains, about anything.

I started introducing music-to-wend-our-way-to-the-bathroom-and-back, last night. And this morning, as we set off for the bathroom again, Mother immediately queried, "Where's our music?"

Kisses,
Ju

◆   ◆   ◆

8th June

Hi Sweetheart,

Cricket's being televised. Australia and England are playing for the Ashes.

I talked with you a couple of hours ago and am very sorry to hear your back is so painful. Do please take care of you.

Kevin just went to spend time with Mother, but she told him she needed to sleep. On his return downstairs, he shared, "I think it is probably only a matter of days."

In my luggage I brought with me a copy of this month's Nature Conservancy magazine, and the centerfold shows the Grand Prize winning photograph of the magazine's annual photography competition. It will be better to show you the picture when I get home, rather than to describe it here. It is uncaptioned. I showed it to Mother and asked her what caption she would give it; without the slightest hesitation, she said, "Into the Silence."

This morning, when I was assisting her in the bathroom, she said, "I can feel it coming, Judith."

"What are you referring to?" I asked.

"Well, *you* know!" she replied.

"Death?"

"Yes … the winning post."

This is not a race I have any heart for her to win and witness my intermittent longing to hang on to her presence. I am so reluctant to let this remarkable woman go, yet I know I cannot be in the way of her leaving. She is so peaceful about it all and somewhat impatient to be on her way. Her readiness is enough. Perhaps her lingering is for the rest of us to learn our last lessons from her, and may be for her to get complete with something, or someone, of which I, and perhaps even she, is as yet unaware.

Change of subject: yesterday, I encountered two people in the High Street and with some amusement noted my response to their diversity. The first was Vincent, the deacon, who gives Mother Communion on Sundays. He was with his wife, though he failed to introduce us. After Vincent and I exchanged pleasantries, and I'd updated him on Mother's condition, I introduced myself to his wife. She said, simply, "I'm Vincent's wife." No name! When I passed on Vincent's heartfelt wishes to Mother, she told me his wife is the local mayor. Such is the subservient, or egoless, role some women fill when in the company of their husbands. The second encounter was with the bookmaker from the betting shop. We talked about the Derby, which was an exquisite race, won by a nose, exchanging our mutually animated interest in the event. I supposed these two diverse encounters might serve to illustrate two aspects of my archetypal character—the warrior woman, and the gambler.

The Derby picnic went brilliantly yesterday. I covered Mother's bed with an Irish linen, embroidered table cloth, which I think Damian gave her years ago. With Mother comfortably propped up with pillows, I prepared her tray with a cream-colored, crisp, linen cloth, and a small vase of purple freesias. Then I carried up her beautiful china, *Belle Fiore*, which she's had for years; silver eating utensils; condiments, and scads, and scads of food; I perched the food on any flat surface I could find. We dined in style, and Kevin popped the champagne cork, while being coached by Mother to, "Go out on the landing, and point it away from the skylight, please, Kevin," and the flutes were filled to the sparkling brim.

We toasted being together and sipped quietly, each with our own thoughts. My throat felt so constricted I could hardly swallow. Sadness and joy all mixed up. Mother's appetite was surprisingly good, and the Derby race superb. I shrieked with excitement, even though your horse, and mine, lost.

5:35 PM

Mother's just finished a supper of chicken soup with small pasta shells. She really enjoyed it, along with a fresh peach, succulent, and juicy.

Today, I guess that in about a week, Mother will leave. Her skin appears slightly tinged with what could be jaundice. I don't know if regular bowel movements and jaundice coincide or not. She is very pleased with herself, now that she is eliminating regularly. She can't stand the thought of being given an enema.

Tonight, she couldn't stand up without assistance, but once she got her balance, we danced to *In the Mood*, all the way to the bathroom and back.

Please take care of your back. I trust you'll do absolutely nothing strenuous until your strain has completely healed. Please ask other able-bodied folk to assist with the heavy lifting for the landscape construction work that you are doing around our Sanctuary.

Thank goodness for the technology of the phone. I just finished talking with Lucie and shared, what was for me, a heart-wrenching good-bye. She knew who I was, though she was barely coherent. I love her dearly. I also spoke with your sisters, our conversation very emotional. My sadness deepens to know Lucie is leaving.

How is it that we are both losing our mothers, at the same time? I bless the fact that you and I connect by voice each day. That, and pouring out the moments of each day to you in letters, is how I am emptied and can remain present to all that life is bringing us. I love you, miss your physical presence, and know you are here in spirit, every second of every day with all of us—just as I am with you, Lucie, Eleanor, and Barbara; life is a continual process of letting go.

Kisses, gentle hugs, and love,
Ju

◆   ◆   ◆

8ᵗʰ June
8:30 PM

Hi Love,

Last night, after I'd posted my letter to you, I stopped in at the City Arms for a pint of ale. It was early, seven-ish. I'd noticed on prior evenings that one of the bartenders spoke with an American accent and, after striking up a conversation, learned he'd grown up in Farmington, New Mexico. His parents are Brits. He has dual nationality and lives here in the village—such a small world.

Today, England won the cricket match against the Australians. Kevin watched with rapt interest. And I've just watched our favorite show, with Judi Dench, *As Time Goes By*, about which Mother advised me earlier, "That program with HB in it is on tonight, Judith." Even in this house you are recognized as looking like the male lead character, Lionel, played by Geoffrey Palmer. I think it was a recent episode, as e-mail was mentioned in it; it was a new episode to me, however, even though it was billed as a rerun. Mother and I enjoyed the flawless performances; the story-line and characters are so appealing; laughter lightened our every moment—another blessing for this day.

Continued on 9th June
8:45 AM

Hi again,

Mother was so weak this morning I didn't think I could move her safely from her bed to the commode. The R.N., who comes in once a week, ordered the commode brought in a few days ago, intended to reduce the number of walks to the bathroom.

This is how we've been managing thus far: I somehow maneuver Mother's body to the edge of the bed and, once I get her legs over the side and her feet on the floor, I hold her firmly supported against my body; then she needs to take one step—as we make a hundred and eighty degree turn—and she holds herself as upright as she can while I use my free hand to pull her nightgown up and her panties and pad down; I then place her carefully on the commode. This is done with us *both* trusting that I won't allow her body to slide to the floor.

At 6:00 AM, I went in to her room. She lay there, looking lovely, and so peaceful, and then announced in a weak voice, "I don't think I can move this morning."

Not knowing if I had the strength to lift her entirely, I thought I'd attempt to use a bit of help from gravity. I asked her if, with my help, she could roll on to her right side and bring her legs over the side of the bed—an enormously difficult task in her weakened state. She managed, and I rolled her from lying on her right side to upright on her bottom—like one of those nesting Babushka dolls—and was then able to lift her to her feet. After I had one-hundred-and-eighty-degreed her body and placed her on the commode, she expressed complete surprise at how easily we managed, and said, "How light I feel now, no aches or pains." Then she declared in a strong voice, "I think I'm getting better!" My heart feels like it is breaking. I love her so.

She has since eaten breakfast, and we danced our way to the bathroom, where she completed her ablutions. Her linen is now changed, and her hair brushed, and it is 10:00 AM, sharp. She is sitting up, coiffed, hairspray and all, waiting for Rachel to arrive and bathe her.

Kevin is making lunch today, and I'm grateful—fried onions, garlic, potatoes and eggs. It sounds like an omelet to me, but he calls it, "A tortilla, Vigo-style."

This morning, I surmise that Kevin is missing teaching as he launched into a long monologue, distinguishing some finer points of the English language; then he proceeded to iterate the many definitions of words of similar pronunciation, and the root of this and that, until I was compelled, by a momentary ennui, to say, "I really don't have quite the same level of interest in this subject as you."

He looked slightly crestfallen as his audience of one evaporated upstairs.

He's visiting Mother now. She will be his captive audience until Rachel comes in an hour. (Oh, I'm wrong—that was a short visit! Mother must have asked Kevin to pick up something from the shops, as he's just trundled down the stairs and left, with the shopping basket over his arm.)

Did I tell you about the new priest, Father Jim? He's tall, though shorter than you, as the top of his abundant, curly, dark brown hair just brushes the light fixture in Mother's sitting room. He's blue-eyed, I think of Irish descent, and brimming with life and laughter. I'd guess he's about thirty-three years of age, which seems young to have a parish of this size. Earlier, he administered the sacrament of Anointing of the Sick to Mother, and then went downstairs to enjoy a glass of Rioja with Kevin and to watch the cricket match for twenty minutes, before departing with a cheery wave.

Mother told me later that according to Father Jim, he, and several fellow-students at Oxford—all from different branches of Christianity—formed a club. These twelve friends still meet as often as possible, and they call themselves the Crewdites. He laughed when he told Mother the name. Mother explained to me, "I must have looked a bit blank, as Father Jim laughed again, and said, "*You know, 'crudités'*, as in the French ... for raw vegetables." So he has a sense of humor, too. Mother recounted how he'd introduced himself to her by saying, "People in the parish kept asking me if I'd been to see Enid yet, and I thought it was high time I came to meet you."

He's only been in the parish two weeks, and told Mother he hasn't unpacked yet. No doubt he's enjoying the many invitations he mentioned, from parishioners of the fairer sex. Mother, *wreathed* in smiles after he'd gone, said in the voice of a young girl, "And he loves to grow ... oh, I've forgotten which flowers he said he loves to grow ... anyway, he's so charming, don't you think?"

Another letter came from you this morning, dated 2nd June. I've received seven in such a short time, and you say you've received none of mine yet! By the time you read this one you'll probably have received six on one day.

Yesterday, I witnessed a persistent wish hanging in my mind that Sándor would call to say good-bye to his grandmother.

Your letters convey that we have finally achieved a *real* country-garden-look at our Sanctuary—overgrown and somewhat casual, yet with a visible semblance of thought given to the plantings. How lovely! Please leave all of its care to me, for when I get home. It will be such a joy to get my fingers back into the good, good earth of the Sanctuary. I'll just dissolve into it. It will be so therapeutic. Just to be there with you, making love, eating healthfully, reading, walking, and seeing family and friends—heaven on earth without a doubt. Oh! I nearly forgot! I do have to go back to work!

I trust your sore back is feeling easier now. Remember that you are loved by me, that your children, and my children, and your sisters, and our dear friends, all love you. I miss your presence, yet I have your support and love with me, at all times, just as you have mine.

Kisses,
Ju

◆   ◆   ◆

Father Jim's visit prompted some reflection on my early years and how religion played a part in my upbringing. I recall the winter Sundays of my childhood when—following the closure of my parent's hotel at the end of the summer season—the six of us would walk the quarter mile to eight o'clock Mass. Ann and I would walk in front, holding hands, followed by our brothers, with our parents in the rear. My father always walked on the curb side, with my mother's arm linked in his. I never saw them hold hands.

My parents were devout Catholics, attending weekly Confession, and taking Communion every Sunday, and sometimes during the week. We children were taught the same disciplines and rituals, and were faithful—until we left home; after which we each stopped practicing, one after another.

My brothers attended a Catholic boys' school, and Ann and I, a convent. My sister and I found the strict religious environment less than palatable, and the thought of subjecting a child of my own to a similar religious education, left me cold. I was still practicing my faith, when—following the birth of my three children in less than three years—my doctor recommended that I use birth control, "... because you need to give your body a rest." I couldn't reconcile continuing to practice my faith, while disobeying one of the Catholic Church's strict rules, so stopped. A deep sense of guilt remained for many years, until I realized that my relationship with Infinity, or God, does not depend on practicing any particular religion.

Mother was deeply saddened by our rejection of her chosen faith. On many of my earlier visits she spoke to me of her disappointment, but had not mentioned it since my most recent arrival.

◆   ◆   ◆

9th June

Hi HB,

It's 6:40 PM and I imagine your massage is over by now. I do hope it was helpful and that your back feels easier.

Eleanor's prognosis for Lucie does not sound hopeful. I am beaming unconditional love Lucie's way, for peace and comfort as she goes, and love, and light, to you, and all the family. Your grief, begun long since, will deepen as she leaves.

I'd prefer to be with you in person at the Memorial Service Eleanor is arranging but, of course, I won't be. I must confess, with abject horror, that I noticed my mind thinking that I'd miss out on three days paid bereavement leave for the death of a mother-in-law. I felt deeply ashamed of the thoughts, just incubating there like a clutch of rotten eggs. So be it.

After I spoke with you earlier, Paul stopped by. Did you ever meet him? He manages the Georgian house for the homeowners here, and is like a one-man board-of-directors. There's an Annual General Meeting tonight, and he said he'll stop in, on either Wednesday or Thursday, to give Mother the latest house news. She's so pleased about that. She wants to stay engaged with what's going on in the house, even as her death approaches.

The landlord of the Globe Inn passed me in the street today and asked how Mother is doing. When we went there for a drink during my last flying visit a few weeks ago, Ann mentioned to him that Mother's health was declining He remembered the circumstances, and me, an amazingly good memory. Is this illustrative of another of my archetypes? To be recognized by, and engaged in conversation with, the deacon, the bookmaker, and a publican, all within three days, seems quite comical. I feel drawn into the community—in less than two weeks! And I suppose, in other times, I might have been drawn in by the butcher, the baker, and the candlestick-maker.

Today has been lovely, some broken cloud, and lots of sunshine. I feel very fortunate to be here in such pleasant weather.

The doctor came in again today. He told Mother he is, "... going on my holidays, to the Scilly Isles ..." (Doesn't that sound like a John Cleese line?) "... leaving on the 14th, and returning to work on the 30th."

After he'd completed his visit with Mother, he padded down the stairs into the sitting room. With the most quizzical expression on his face, he looked first at Kevin, and then at me, and said, "I've never had a patient say *anything* like that to me before," and continued in an incredulous tone, "When I told your mother I was going away and would be back on the 30th, she said, 'We'd better say good-bye then, Doctor, because I won't be here when you get back.' And when I told her I thought that she would *indeed* still be here, she looked up at me and said, most emphatically, 'Damn!'" He laughed aloud as he left, saying, "What an amazing woman!"

He also told us we shall be dealing with his locum while he's gone. Ann likes the locum and even more importantly, so does Mother. So, unless Infinity and Mother come to some other agreement, I'll be here well into July, and will need to extend my leave.

With that in mind, I called the office this afternoon and spoke with my manager, Nicole. She told me the meeting that I'd spent months designing, and organizing, went very well. "They did all but hold hands and sing Kum Bi Ya," were her exact words; she is so comical. She also gave me an update on last week's department meeting, to keep me "… in touch." I find, though, that I have absolutely no interest in work at all, right now. I told her that according to the doctor, Mother will most likely be here for a few more weeks, and she said, "Do what you need to do." It is such a relief to have a supportive manager.

After Mother's 8:00 PM medication and her penultimate trip to the bathroom for the day, I shall go out to the pub for a pint of ale. It is so replenishing to sit alone in the City Arms courtyard for thirty minutes, just being still.

I love you immeasurably, until my heart overflows—it is so full, and deep, and infinite.

Kisses, hugs and love, always,
Ju

P.S. I'll save this to add to tomorrow, as I have a sixty-three pence stamp left, and can write one or two more pages to make up the weight. I'm out of forty-three pence stamps, for now.

7:40 PM

A single blackbird is perched on the wall below Mother's bedroom window, its head is raised, and joy exudes through its infinitely beautiful song—breathtakingly lovely. I don't know of another birdsong that touches my spirit as deeply.

Plus, the sun is streaming through the windows, filling the room with golden light—a moment of pure astonishment!

Continued on 10th June

Hello love, dearest HB:

An infinite abundance of love always, especially on this our eighth anniversary.

I arose at 6:00 AM; Mother was sound asleep and remained so until 7:00, when I woke her to take the first pills of the day. She informed me she feels well, and rested.

By 9:15 AM, all the morning administrations—medications, ablutions, breakfast—were complete (at least what I do). Then Ann arrived to visit with Mother for a while.

Gwen, the district nurse, has come and gone already—to get an egg-crate, air-mattress, which is intended to avoid the development of bed sores. A new commode—this one *on wheels*— will be delivered today, so when Mother's legs give out completely we will still be able to make our journey to the bathroom.

Mother's doctor informed me that, "… nearer the end, a catheter and enemas may be necessary."

I can't think how the result of an enema will be disposed of with Mother lying in bed, but I'm sure somebody knows. The logistics of such things will unfold, and I'll learn as the need arises; however, if Mother has any say, and she will, none of that will occur.

Gwen has returned with the air-mattress. As I write, she is inflating it with a pump. When Rachel comes, she and Gwen will install the mattress over the existing one.

Kevin is shopping.

I make coffee for everyone who comes in. That's what I'm doing now, between writing sentences to you. From this you can tell it gets busy around here.

When Rachel arrives (and she just has) she, Gwen, and Mother, will have their coffee with an apple tart. Then lunch preparations will start.

I love you, infinitely, in each moment,

Ju

◆   ◆   ◆

The practical aspects of caring for my mother came very easily to me as, when I was a young mother of three children under three years of age, I had learned to create order out of what could be quite chaotic situations. I was totally committed to being in service to Mother's every need and, at the same time, tend to my own need for nurture, personal space, and staying fully present. I had not mastered the latter during early motherhood!

To this end, within a day or two of arriving, I made a list of Mother's medications, with the prescribed dosage and times of administration, and taped it to the refrigerator. Next, I consciously created a mental picture of the daily routine and, as another task was added, or Mother's needs changed, or the health care providers prescribed something new, I adjusted the picture accordingly. Periodically, throughout each day, I did a mental check that everything was being covered, and with this structure prevailing, I could surrender to the stillness within, and hold my heart open.

This combination—of structure and surrender—allowed me to be present to my mother; listening deeply, understanding her needs and wants, witnessing her grace and the dignity with which she lived, fully, in each moment. In her presence, I felt humbled by her *being* and deeply privileged to be supporting her. There was an ease to being with her that was lost only when my mind butted in with its insistent chattering—dwelling either on the past, or conjecturing about the future; the latter was an instant cue to surrender again, to the present moment, and be at peace with what is.

◆   ◆   ◆

11th June

Dearest HB,

It's Wednesday, 1:45 PM, and I want to get this off to you before the 3:30 post. My body is enjoying its first sit down since 6:45 AM; Kevin and Mother are napping.

I've written two cards for Mother today. One to my children's father, who thoughtfully and generously sent an *enormous* floral arrangement with a card, saying, "Enid, you are in my thoughts."

Mother was deeply touched by the flowers, and when she read his note, her face flushed a deep pink. She asked me to write for her, "A very humble note of thanks, please," then added that as she'd said, only two days ago, that she's not humble enough to go yet, "God is giving me another opportunity to practice some more."

At first, she'd asked me to compose the note for her, but I refused, saying, "This is *your* note. What do *you* want to say to him?"

In a voice filled with profound humility, tears of emotion welling-up, she softly, and haltingly, dictated: "Forgive me, for my twenty years of silence."

Quite unbidden, tears spilled down my cheeks. I am so filled with respect and admiration for her. She opened her heart without hesitation, seizing the moment, to complete another unfinished communication with someone she loved, but had not spoken with since our divorce.

Then Mother asked me to write a note of thanks to Rachel, for all her attentions this last year, and gave me instructions to take a taxi to Browne's nursery to pick up two climbing roses, called Compassion, for Rachel's garden—more closure, expressed with loving gratitude.

Last night, Mother talked again about her relationship with God, and she supposed that as she, "... can't seem to pray any more ..." perhaps a different kind of communication might be appropriate. She seemed comforted by this self-revelation. Today, she said, quite assuredly, "I *expect* to go to heaven," which was followed immediately with a half-suppressed, horrified gasp, coupled with an embarrassed giggle, as she added, "Now *that* isn't very humble, is it?"

Oh, how I love this woman!

I gently suggested that she just *trusts*, then, rather whimsically, I began to recite the Ten Commandments (I couldn't remember the fourth, but Mother filled me in when I hesitated), and after I'd recited the tenth, I asked her, "So how many of these have you broken lately?"

"None," she replied, emphatically.

"Well, you might consider asking for forgiveness for any venial sins and, when the time comes, hold on to your tummy for the rocketing ascent."

She reached for my hand, laughing so lightheartedly, and we laughed together; the little dimple under her right eye deepening. Perhaps that's what's in her way; she does seem afraid of going to hell, and isn't quite sure she's going to heaven, at least until she feels humble enough.

The whole concept of physical places called heaven and hell—other than what we consciously, or unconsciously, create for ourselves right here on earth—seems strange to me, yet I respect how deeply Mother's beliefs are an integral part of her. Throughout her life, her faith has been a source of great strength. May it be now, and continue to be so, throughout her remaining days.

A little chuckle for you at my egotistical assumptions—when the florist's van pulled up with the flowers from my children's father, I said to Kevin, "Oh good! These will be for me, from HB. It's our anniversary!"

Then I went to the door, and gushed, "Flowers, for me?"

"No. They're for your mother," the delivery man replied, laconically. (The florists in the village know her well).

And I smiled to myself, knowing I'd have this little tale to tell you. Kevin kindly made no comment!

All is well here. Mother is asleep upstairs, her room a deluge of flowers. Kevin, after demolishing a huge lunch, naps on the settee, and the love of your life is off to the Post Office.

I'm so happy for Sándor. He called Mother last night and expressed his love for her, and she the same to him—another completion. He told me that he and his friend (he's pretty sure she's coming with him) are arriving at the Sanctuary on 2nd July, and returning home on 7th July. I'm so delighted.

I love you sweetheart, kisses,
Ju

◆   ◆   ◆

12th June
6:00 AM

Dearest Love,

I wept all the way home from our phone call yesterday, and lay awake for hours last night thinking of dear departed Lucie. What intention she had, to consciously refuse food and fluids, knowing she would die of dehydration. (Such power we humans have, when our intention is clear, and we surrender to it.) How perfect for her that your sisters and other caregivers honored her Living Will, and she died at home in her own bed, without any unwanted intervention.

She had such a full life. I lay awake recollecting the stories she modestly eked out when we visited her on the Cape. Her high school basketball prowess; her lifelong friendship with Clara (their spirits no doubt shooting hoops as I write); teaching; marrying your Dad; sailing down Maine each summer in her father-in-law's sail boats; having three great kids she loved so; travelling the world over, and living a good comfortable life—with your Dad when he was living, and since he died.

She so generously accepted me into the family. My heart fills with love for her, and I weep at the loss of her physical presence on this earth. As you told me, she had some sorrows, though she never spoke of them in my hearing—her mother's long illness, and perhaps some fears she shared with you. She was such a private person.

Through the fifteen years or so that I knew her, she was always affectionate, with a sharp, quick wit. I remember how she loved to drive with you on the Cape, gunk-holing about from harbor to harbor; the day trips off the Cape with Eleanor, and listening to Barbara's beautiful coloratura soprano in church. She loved you, her children, so much, and she was so happy for us. We shall talk about her for the rest of our lives, with love, humor, and respect. Lucie, your physical presence is missed, in every moment.

Both Ann and Enid send their condolences and love to you, and ask that you please convey their kind thoughts to all the family at the Memorial Service. When I told her last night that Lucie died, Mother frowned and said, "I'm quite cross that Lucie beat me to it!" I didn't know whether to laugh or cry.

My love to you, take special care of yourself. Allow everyone, who is willing and able, to support you in their own way. I imagine their expressions of love for you will vary on a continuum from silence, to voiced compassion, to unintended intrusiveness.

Kisses, hugs, and always, love,
Ju

◆   ◆   ◆

13th June
11:00 AM

Hello my Love,

Lying in bed this morning, I thought how nice it would be to come into your room and snuggle up in bed with you.

It's usually about 5:00 AM when I wake, though sometimes earlier, as dawn begins to lighten the sky a little before 4:00. On the 21st, the daylight hours begin decreasing by minutes, and seconds. Summer solstice is nigh.

Mother is in good spirits today. On first rising, she was a bit dizzy and none too steady on her feet, yet I managed to get her onto and off the commode without incident. After breakfast, I hummed *In the Mood* as we wheeled off to the bathroom for her private time. En route, I leaned the commode chair back a little, and gently jigged it from side-to-side, in time with the beat. Mother made little foot-tapping movements on the foot rests, and I stopped briefly at our reflection in the mirror on the landing. She smiled up at me, her head to one side, and joined me in the tune until I parked her at the washbasin. Such is her light-heartedness.

I managed to bathe before writing to you today, so feel like there is a little extra time. (What an illusion!) With Mother safely back in bed I stayed in my room and read for one uninterrupted hour—such luxury.

Kevin's gone grocery shopping. Rachel has arrived; she's later than usual as she has also picked up Hazel's workload, as the latter is on holiday until Monday.

Yesterday, my mind's impatience to be with you kept rearing its ugly head and, by nightfall, I even felt sporadic feelings of resentment about my choice to be here. Despite surrendering to those, I still witnessed some intermittent, intrusive impatience to be home with you—horrific selfishness; I'm just missing our mealtimes and quiet hours, and working on our place, together. I am so fortunate to have your unconditional love, and true acceptance of who I am. And ... I feel equally fortunate to be here, with Mother, caring for her from that inner source of strength—stillness.

By the time you read this, you'll be at your son Stephen's home, in Massachusetts, preparing for Lucie's Memorial Service. I trust you'll be at peace with what is and soak up spending time with your three children. Give my love to Eleanor and Barbara, and all their family members—and, of course, your children.

It boggles my mind that you'll be with your three children and then with mine, all within a couple of weeks—such rare occasions. How many years do you suppose it will be before that occurs again, and on what occasion? It'll be a long while before my three get together again, when I too, can be with them.

Again, give everyone my love and a warm hug,

I love you, HB.
Ju

◆   ◆   ◆

14th June
9:45 AM

Hi dear HB,

Two letters came from you today. Kisses and hugs for them both.

I rose at 6:45. How I miss our shower! These ancient English homes with only tubs don't quite do it for me. Yet, remembering the Saturday nights of my early childhood, when my mother filled the tin tub before the fire ... I'm grateful for this tub.

Kevin is out, shopping for salmon filets to poach for lunch, and I'm with you for a few minutes.

After taking care of Mother this morning, making her breakfast; her bed; doing light ablutions, and brushing her hair, she is now reading in bed. She says her eyesight must be declining as the printed page is blurry. She is much weaker, today. She can't do much with her left arm, as if her muscles atrophied overnight, though her grip still feels quite strong. She greeted me with, "It's funny, you know, this morning I don't feel a bit as though I'm dying!"

And this, after being so weak, exhausted, and short of breath last night.

I'm remembering that the frequent mood swings I'm experiencing are all connected to the stages of grief. When I forget, I judge myself for having any negative feelings at all—like being impatient and feeling resentful—which just compounds the negativity. But then I remember the stages, and I recoup, and know it is all natural, and surrender again; I'm at peace and present.

Paul came in yesterday afternoon and visited Mother for an hour. They laughed and laughed, enjoying a good gossip about the Annual General Meeting—who said what, which decisions were made, under which house rules.

Then Ann went up to visit Mother for two hours, and when I took Mother's supper up at 5:15, they appeared to be enjoying a nice chat; however, when Ann came downstairs, she said, in a somewhat strangled voice, "Mother *thanked* me!" And quickly gathering her things, she left for home.

When I went up later for Mother's tray, she commented that Ann's visit went well, but indicated nothing out of the ordinary. Perhaps she managed to reach closure with Ann, as well. How wonderful if she did.

It's sunny and bright today, a few white puffs of cloud. It's cool enough to wear a couple of layers, pleasant, though a bit on the chilly side.

While Paul and Ann were visiting Mother, Kevin and I sat in the living room. While I read, he used a magnifying glass to pour over a pictorial history of the village, which he'd bought Mother years ago, and is taking back to Spain with him. He also read the Radio Times/TV Guide. This morning, he said that the latter publication could be used to give someone a complete education, and added that he's also taking home last week's edition as well.

I asked if he meant a complete education *in English*, which seemed vaguely possible, as that's what he teaches, and his reply came imperiously, "No. I said a *complete education.*"

I didn't ask him to elucidate. Our paradigms don't overlap in too many places.

Rachel's due in at 11:00, to bathe Mother. I'm so glad she and Hazel are willing to come in on Saturdays as well now. Perhaps they won't mind adding one or two Sundays, which will be better for Mother, as they do a much more competent job of bathing her than I. Somehow, we'll have to work Sunday bathing around the deacon's visit.

I love you, kisses and hugs,
Ju

◆   ◆   ◆

When we gathered to be with our mother during her final weeks, there were many opportunities for me to deepen my knowledge and understanding of my siblings, though I do know Ann far better than either of our brothers, having spent more time with her throughout our adult lives.

Ann, well-traveled in her youth, rode pillion, in her late teens and early twenties, behind a motor-bicycling boyfriend; they spent summer after summer, cruising around Europe.

She excelled in her career—behind-the-scenes in the television industry—until her mid-thirties, when the frightening symptoms of agoraphobia ended her career. Despite the symptoms, she pushed herself to hike the mountains of Wales, in training for the ascent to Mt. Everest's base camp, where she and her husband spent their honeymoon. Her husband was part of the filming crew of the British expedition's successful ascent that year, and the expedition members, including Ann, were honored with an invitation to Buckingham Palace. They were presented to Queen Elizabeth and Prince Philip, and to the Prime Minister, at #10 Downing Street.

Notwithstanding the many life challenges with which Ann has been faced, she has overcome them all, through sheer determination and tenaciousness, and she now immerses herself in an independent, private, and secluded life. She revels in classical music, and devours books on history, humor, and biographies of interest. She occasionally expresses a transient desire to live somewhere other than England, but she is a true Brit, loyal and patriotic, though not always in agreement with the national politicians, or their alliances.

Over the many years we have lived apart, she and I have enjoyed a close relationship, mostly via the telephone, and have spent many vacations together, in England. It is important to us both to stay in close touch—though we hold differing views on most subjects, and contrast greatly in personality. Ann enjoys being in familiar surroundings with an established routine, while I, since retirement, continue to move from place to place with HB, and gladly change plans, or direction, on a whim.

Damian, on the other hand—having left England for Europe at about the same time I left for the United States—has scant time for his place of birth. He has retired to the coast of Spain now, and enjoys his life there with TA, and a community of close friends. After he left England, he stayed in touch with Mother on a regular basis, and generously contributed to her income, for which she frequently expressed her gratitude.

In our young adulthood, Damian and I enjoyed a correspondence for many years, but over time our letters petered out, and it was only when I took an assignment in Geneva for a couple of years, and became his neighbor, that we renewed our relationship, and updated our friendship and knowledge of one another. Damian has a keen interest in people, and has the capacity to listen intently, without interrupting (a trait neither I, nor Kevin, employ with any great skill). A world traveler, Damian's knowledge of languages, cultures, and geography, seemingly has no end—though he is never boastful, exhibiting modesty reminiscent of our mother's; absent her pride. He has tremendous passion, which lies dormant until something or someone sparks it, when it flies forth, accompanied by wild hand and arm gesticulations, and his voice rises in volume and feeling. He and I have grown very fond of one another in our later years.

By the time Kevin flew to England to be with Mother in her last weeks, he'd lived in Spain for a dozen years or so. He and I rarely corresponded, so most of what I knew of his life came to me secondhand, from Mother, or Ann. Since living in Spain, Kevin spent his annual vacations visiting Mother.

He fears flying, though he does his best to conceal it, thus he prefers to travel by train, bus and ferry—the journey from Spain to England taking an arduous forty-eight hours. His visits to the U.K. coincided with mine only once, so our scant firsthand knowledge of each other's lives was conveyed via birthday and Christmas cards. We shared perhaps no more than half-a-dozen phone calls over the years, though, with the advent of e-mail, our contact has increased dramatically in recent years.

Of my siblings, I know Kevin least well, though I recognize myself in him more readily than in Ann, or Damian. Kevin and I are strongly opinionated, self-confident; quick to interrupt, and slow to apologize. My observations of his behavior, when we were together at Mother's home for so many weeks, offered me a sobering reflection of my own.

It was at Mother's that I listened to Kevin's avuncular sentiments for the culture and people of Galicia, where he now lives, and where he has settled into the local community with great ease. He has established, what is for him, a satisfying life of teaching, writing, researching, and enjoying the gastronomic delights of neighborhood restaurants, and cafés.

During those days and weeks with my brothers at our mother's home, there was a dearth of conversation between us about our individual experience, or feelings, about Mother's impending death. What was there to say out loud that each did not already sense? Without a word said, my siblings and I understood the chasm of loss each felt. And that, coupled with the stiff-upper-lip-syndrome, palpable in our family culture for generations, evidenced itself in our silence. We worked around each other's personal space, intuitively respecting and accommodating each other's sensibilities as best we could, and placing all of our attention on Mother, as the days moved us inexorably towards her death.

On the other hand, my sister and I were quick to take advantage of the few evenings we spent together at the pub, where I listened to her express feelings of anticipated loss, loneliness, and anxiety about her future. She needed my ear and my empathy; I was happy to be there for her. Whereas, I continued to surrender to my roller-coasting emotions in the privacy of my inner world, and in every letter home—where I felt free to empty my mind and release erupting tensions; my eternal gratitude to HB.

During those weeks—and even more deeply since—I realized that there is no *right* way to behave at such a time, no *right* way to communicate with one another; however we behaved, everyone was doing their best to support Mother, and one another, in the only way we knew how—no matter what it looked or sounded like, in the moment.

◆   ◆   ◆

15th June
Just after midnight.

Hello HB,

I've some thoughts on caring for the dying: the most challenging aspects of it—especially when one is unaccustomed to it—is finding the stillness within, and leaving oneself out of the equation.

To be *present* every second of every minute, every hour, every day, means being aware of the other's bodily needs as though they were one's own. For example, the need to urinate, the need to defecate, the need for medications—for pain, for nausea, for regularity, for sleep. The need to eat and drink, to have clean linen, nightgown, pants, pad, to have pillows adjusted, sit up, lie down, turn over, clean teeth, wash hands, have a clean, hygienic home, to grocery shop, water the plants, deadhead the flowers—and so on, and on—*being* the daily routine of another's body, and life.

Being their structure, as though it were one's own—structure that each of us has in our own lives, under some semblance of conscious (or unconscious) routine and order. It is astonishing, the *alertness* and *presence* needed to keep releasing my attachments and aversions, so that they don't impede the serving of Mother's needs.

This *alert presence* is allowing me to be her physical structure, and at the same time, *be with her*, fully, in every moment. When I *am* present it just flows, yet I still want to be aware of my own experience. That's the challenge, to *be with her* totally and yet, in the same moment, witness and experience, fully, my feelings of deepest sorrow at losing her, and my joy at having the privilege of being in service to her.

That's what I'm doing here, or I should say *being* here—the structure upon which Enid's quality of life, as well as the peacefulness of her death, somewhat depends. It is no different than the role of a parent caring for an infant, or what an attendant does in service to someone with quadriplegia. An infant, and some-one with quadriplegia, need the same total physical care. Here, that attention is provided sixteen hours a day now.

According to the doctor, Mother can have a night nurse for four to five hours, so I am offered the choice of some uninterrupted rest; however, Mother wants me to be with her when she dies, so I'll not avail myself of that extra service. It's all working well, and I feel utterly privileged to be invited in to her life in this way.

Tonight, she could not put any weight on her feet. I needed to support her body completely as we made that one step from bed to commode. Just she and I watched horse racing from York in her room this afternoon. She ate a great breakfast, lunch, and supper.

Take care of you. I'll continue this later today.

Kisses,
Ju

◆   ◆   ◆

Reflecting further on the topic of the last letter, I can say, unabashedly, that it never occurred to me that I would not be able to perform the role of caring for my mother. Not knowing *how* to do it didn't deter me. I was committed to be there for her, and I trusted the process to unfold.

Like many other new mothers, I became the primary caregiver to my first child without any prior experience of child care. I imagined that caring for a dying parent would take the same vigilance, though I was fully aware that the emotional content would differ.

The previous year, when Mother got herself discharged from the hospital a week earlier than the doctor planned, I recall my momentary dread and doubt, about my capacity to emotionally absorb all that was to come, yet *be with her* in the way that she needed, moment-to-moment. That moment of dread, and another, at the time of her phone call, informing me it was "time to come," were the only moments of self-doubt that I recall.

We had prepared well, however: Mother, by getting her affairs in order, and I, by recognizing the two certain pitfalls that I would encounter when I was with her at the end—dwelling in regret about the past (regarding the many lost years of her company), and dwelling in emotional anxiety about her impending death.

Knowing these challenges and feeling Mother's unwavering trust in me was one source of strength. But, would my feelings and thoughts get in the way of being present to her needs? I didn't know. That was only revealed as each moment unfolded.

◆   ◆   ◆

Same day
9:45 AM

Hi Love,

It's a beautiful day, clear and sunny.

This is the time Mother sleeps for a short while—after commode use, breakfast, bathroom ablutions, and a wee chat. I've bathed, vacuumed, and dusted. Communion is on the way, via the deacon, and Rachel is coming to bathe Mother.

This morning, Mother remarked, "I've been thinking. What if I *never* balance my karma? How dreadful! I'll keep coming back for thousands of years!"

I thought about this for a while, then offered, "I read somewhere that what balances one's karma is true forgiveness, for oneself, and for all others in one's life, for whom one thinks forgiveness is necessary."

Her reply came in a small, soft voice, "How hard it is to forgive myself, *and* others!" Then she looked up, and with great determination, said, "But I'll do it."

I commented out loud—for our mutual benefit—how arrogant it is of us not to forgive ourselves when, (in her faith), God forgives us when we ask. We victimize ourselves so. Who are we to state that we're not forgivable when we know, from all we've learned (in her faith) that we are? She appeared to be contemplating when I left her.

In answer to an earlier query, she said she feels, "… very well, though physically weaker on my legs. But I'm more alert than yesterday, don't you think? And I feel more strength in my left arm."

Kevin has gone out for a while, and when I was vacuuming downstairs my mind spun out of here, and I found myself thinking how much I'd like to be chatting with you in person. I miss your presence, immeasurably. Our mortality has me grieving at the thought of losing you, yet I do know our spirits will always be together. Hmm! I may go before you! And here I am, off in the future *again*—as though it existed.

When I return home I shall look for all the ways I can be with you even more. To have whole days with you, when we can just *be*. What luxury! Not doing chores unless we feel like it, puttering about while being within sight or hailing distance of one another. We could drive to Colorado, or Utah, or Arizona, or California; to Montana, and Oregon, and Washington. Take a boat into Puget Sound and go to the islands, and walk about gently, and sip fine wine, and eat delicious food—all this, with you. That will be so lovely! Even as my mind takes me, yet again, into the future, I dwell in our love filling every now.

The bells of St. Cuthbert's rang this morning, and I immediately pictured my father, with a group of other local men, all furthering their knowledge of campanology at this very church. I imagine him now, in spirit, listening to the bells along with me, waiting for Mother's energy to merge with his, into the infinite energy that is.

The village is bustling with life. Yesterday, there were dozens of undulating crocodiles of children, each group represented by a different school uniform. They window-shopped their chattering way up the High Street. The Market Square was chock-a-block with hundreds of milling tourists from France, and the cathedral green is sporting booths all around its perimeter. Some of the booth attendants are hawking food and drinks, while others call out appeals for donations to designated charities.

When I stopped to linger for a few seconds, I noticed scads of children, and men and women—some of the latter surely over seventy—participating in *Dancing on the Green*, an annual traditional fête in the village. I watched with delight as the pipers piped, and the Morris dancers leapt about in their white and green costumes; their bells jingling; their sticks slapping, and their handkerchiefs fluttering—such a marvelous English spectacle. The place was mobbed.

After speaking with you on the phone the first time, I strolled to the China and Glass shop, to check on Bartholomew (a.k.a., Barty). He'd left on his afternoon walk with his mistress and has (I heard) completely recovered from his surgery, and is just being his venerable nine-year-old-golden-retriever self. (Thank you for taking care of dear, golden Ollie.)

Kevin suggested brightly, that "Mother is doing so very well indeed, she just may recover completely," at which I witnessed an instant knee-jerk thought, "Oh, no! I don't want to do this, again!"

Aren't reactive thoughts amazing, they way they pop up, unbidden? I actually shook my head to dispel them, but there they lay, another clutch of rotten eggs.

Mother is clearly not comfortable in her faith at the moment; she may choose to linger longer than the doctor predicted, until she finds its center again; I'll ask her if she would like Father Jim to come in for a chat.

I forget if I told you about asking Mother if she hopes, or expects, to "see" her parents, or Phil, in the afterlife. She was momentarily startled by the question, but her answer came readily enough, as she replied, with such vehemence, "The *only* ones I'd like to see again are my friends from Art School. I don't want to see anyone else *at all.*"

Her response may give her pause to ponder on any vestiges of resentment she's still holding; and then again, it may not.

From a somewhat eccentric perspective, I wonder if Mother is trying to live up to an old family script, "If a job's worth doing, it's worth doing right." (From an early age, both our parents taught us that this was the "correct" way to approach work and life.) In the last few days, Mother has acknowledged that she has considerable pride and fleeting humility. And pride, being one of the seven deadly sins, just might give her pause to question whether she is doing this right. And until she achieves the sentiments of "Blessed are the Meek" to her satisfaction, which I venture might require fully accepting her humanness with deep humility, she may just hang on.

About her fleeting humility—a couple of days ago she evacuated her bowels three times (we cut back on the laxative after that) and after the third time, she said, "It is such an *imposition.*"

At first, my egocentric reaction was: how sweet, she's thinking of me—because there's so much cleaning up to do each time—but wisely, I checked the assumption, and asked her, "Imposition? On whom?"

She frowned indignantly, "On *me!*"

She's not at peace with her humanness yet, not in her body, nor in her spirit.

I'm reading the last of Dirk Bogarde's six autobiographical works. It's a delight. He appears to give his all in this one, digging for his own truth and honesty, and sharing more deeply about his personal life than in his other autobiographical works. I respect him so much as an actor, and it feels good to expand that to include his humanity.

It also feels good to reach out and touch *you*, even if it is 3:20 AM there, and you're in the land of nod, perhaps dreaming of us, as I am aware I do—alongside the deep engagement of my heart here.

I love you,
Ju

◆   ◆   ◆

16th June
Monday
11:30 AM

Hi HB,

Another letter came, today, bless your thoughtfulness. Thank you, love.

This morning Mother's urine contained traces of blood. She also informed me that her eyesight is not good. The R.N. insists the latter is caused by the medication.

After the usual morning ablutions, I went to weed the outside edge of Mother's patio wall, and was happy to see—and leave untouched—the small, delicate, wild flowers, and tall, swaying valerian. The weeding took me two hours, though I weeded it in April when I was here. The next time it needs weeding, it may be done by someone else. Yet, I suspect it might be me, if the care Mother continues to enjoy achieves the astounding results evident so far.

Hazel came in, full of smiles, her eyes sparkling, and her hands plunged deep into her cardigan pockets. Her flat, rubber-soled shoes make no sound as she climbs the stairs. She's back from her fortnight's holiday and is sporting a very smart tan. Mother was so pleased to see her, giving her two, big, separate hugs. Mother does have her favorites and, of all who come from the care service, Hazel and Rachel are clearly her favorites.

Kevin went shopping earlier. He continues to enjoy the pictorial history of the village and is using the magnifying glass to discern the minutia buried in the sepia grains. He has started to photograph the same places in the village that are depicted in the book, and is looking forward to comparing them, for their similarities and differences, once he gets back to Spain.

It's a lovely, sunny, scuddy-cloud kind of day; the temperature, pleasant. The laundry is in the machine; the spuds are on.

I have some anger again today, at everyone. I'm aware of my abrupt tone and unwillingness to join in any conversation. It's for nothing of course—just one of the stages. Now that I've noticed it, I realize I'm using it to create some space around me, and will let it go when I go out for some air.

More after lunch!

1:45 PM

The R.N. came. Mother asked her to assist her out of bed and on to the commode. When the R.N. emptied the commode, she neglected to wash it out and traces of blood-stained urine remained. She said nothing to me about it. That's twice today that Mother has passed blood-stained urine; she isn't aware of it. I'll let the doctor know.

Lunch is over—cold, roasted chicken. I'm cooking chicken soup now, prepared from the almost-naked carcass. It's simmering on low, and I'm going up to give Mother a commode-break then I'll come and talk with you, by phone. Clouds have rolled in and it is very overcast—I'll take the umbrella with me.

Kisses and hugs, both gentle and strong,
Ju

◆   ◆   ◆

16th June
8:45 PM

Dearest HB,

After speaking with you briefly on the phone, I took your supportive suggestion and went to the City Arms for some peace and space. With my sense of presence renewed I was pleased to see Ann coming to join me. Thirty minutes and half a pint of ale later, we left to give Mother her 8:00 PM medication.

It's an interesting contrast, to hear Kevin say, "Mother could still get completely better," and to hear Ann say, "Mother's going! You know she's going, at any minute!" In their reality they are both right. And somewhere else is what is.

Mother asked me tonight, "Judith, I want you to stay in touch with Ann, please—I'm asking you to do that for me."

She went on to say that Ann believes that none of us (her siblings) will ever come to England again. "You won't abandon her, will you?" Mother added, with a pleading, anxious expression.

I assured her that I love Ann dearly, and have already told Ann, quite clearly, that I shall come to see her every year, as long as my finances and health permit.

"Oh good," said Mother, sounding very relieved. She cares so about Ann's well-being.

All these brief conversations with Mother are ways for her to come to closure—and me of course! At the end of each day, I recognize how many steps she's taken. Her thoughtful, cautious character appears to be creating a transition that is comfortable for her to manage. On the other hand, it seemed natural for my father—a dominant character if ever there was one—to go decisively, and immediately, with a heart attack.

As I write, I'm in 'my' little bedroom. Today's laundry hangs on the clothes horse, and is draped on the radiator, and on hangers behind the door, and on the outside of the wardrobe door. It's still light, at 9:00 PM, and will be for another forty-five minutes. Kevin is downstairs watching TV and nursing a beer. Mother is doing her best to read a large-print book, loaned by one of the auxiliary nurses.

Today has felt long, and I'm looking forward to putting my head down as soon as I've administered the 10:00 medications. St. Cuthbert's clock is striking the hour, and as I'm writing, I'm aware that my mind is intermittently planning tomorrow's menus! When he telephoned tonight, Mother told Damian that she never remembers eating so well. I noticed my halo squeezing a little.

A difficult challenge here is the lack of space, the confinement of a small village, having no car, and so many comings and goings. Mother's sixty-plus-year-pattern of motherly alertness, to any possible sickness of her offspring, is still active. I blew my nose twice today, and it took several minutes to convince her that "I *do not* have a cold. No, really, I do *not* have a cold!"

The gift, of course, is the sheer joy and delight of having this time with her. The simplicity, honesty, love, acceptance, and just who we are together, will never cease to be a source of wonder and gratitude.

By the time you get this letter you will have spent a week with your children; for the sake of the living, the ritual of honoring the dead will have been completed, and you and your children will have shared a special time together. I hope everything went peacefully for you, and you are getting some rest.

I love you. Be well. Take care of you, for you, and me.
Ju

◆　　　◆　　　◆

Perhaps sorrow about Ann's lifelong feelings of abandonment prompted Mother to ask me to stay in touch with Ann—that and her suspicion that Damian and Kevin held little or no compassion for Ann's years of suffering with agoraphobia. My brothers never acknowledged the condition as "real" and seemed not to understand how it affected Ann's life, as outwardly she appeared to be completely well. Agoraphobia is an insidious condition, indiscernible until symptoms of a panic attack are in full flood. Damian and Kevin never witnessed such an attack. I saw one once, when Ann and Mother came to stay for a few weeks after my father died. That was the first time I observed the severity of the symptoms, and how debilitating and frightening a panic attack is to the person experiencing it.

Ann's pain, at her brothers' perceived lack of care, may have been at the root of her belief that none of her siblings would come to England again, after our mother's death. But this is all conjecture on my part.

◆　　　◆　　　◆

Same evening 10:30 PM

Hi Love,

I want to jot down what just happened before it evaporates in my need for sleep and the surge of my emotions.

At 10:00 I went in to Mother's room to give her the last commode-break of the day and to administer her medication. She was sleeping, propped up on her pillows and looking beautiful. When I enter her room the floor creeks and usually wakes her, as it did tonight.

As I helped her into position on the commode I was moved to refer to her request that I stay in touch with Ann, and said, "Earlier, I heard you release any feelings of responsibility for Ann that you've held on to for so long. Is that right?"

She reached for me and clung tight, kissing my neck, and said a breathless, and heartfelt, "Thank you, I thought I'd dreamed it—but you *heard* me."

I smiled gently, saying, "Yes, I heard you."

She started weeping, and kissed me again, saying, "Thank you, Judith!"

Then we got on with the use of the commode, and taking medication, and when I put her into bed she didn't ask me to place the pillow, just so, as usual. She's just lying there, relaxed, in a completely different position from all previous nights. She pulled me down to her and kissed me again, and looking right into my soul, she said, "Good-bye, dear," (as she does most nights) and for the first time, I replied, "Good-bye, Mother. Sleep peacefully." And I left her.

I'm drawn to sit in her room, and drawn to go to bed and let her be.

9:15 AM
Tuesday

17th June

And there she was at 6:45 this morning, lying peacefully wide awake. She said she awoke at 6:00, and greeted me cheerfully, with, "I had a wonderful night."

Kevin took her a cup of tea, apparently unaware that Mother cannot sit up by herself. For the first time, he had to lift her into a sitting position, and stack the pillows behind her, so she could drink her tea in relative comfort. "He was a bit nonplussed," Mother told me later. He must realize now that Mother has *no* strength.

After breakfast, I bathed her in her bed, followed by a trip to the bathroom to shampoo her hair. She said she feels quite safe and at ease, sitting in the wheeled commode chair with her head over the basin.

Two boxes of Good Earth tea came today. Thank you so much! Plus a lovely letter for Mother and our family. It included the announcement of Lucie's death and her obituary from the Cape Cod newspaper. Mother appreciated getting both. She sends her love to you and is sleeping as I write.

You leave for the Cape today, and I must be sure to phone you before you leave for the airport. It sounds like Eleanor has made good arrangements for everyone to stay close-by.

Ascot races start today, so I'm going to have a bet or two. It's the biggest racing event of the year for the wealthy socialites. The fashions are an important aspect of the spectacle, so the televising starts early, to capture all the society attendees in their finery. Mother really enjoys watching the fashion parade and, no doubt, she will make lots of comments about which fashions are, "Just right!" and which fashions are "Ridiculous!" Despite her failing eye sight!

I'm off to catch the post and do a bit of grocery shopping. Take care of you. Please don't overdo, look after your back.

I love you, HB.
Ju

◆   ◆   ◆

In our mother's last weeks, my behavior and that of my siblings differed broadly. Ann—who for the prior twenty years was Mother's chief support and practically daily visitor—was relieved to take a back seat to the primary role I now performed. She was happy to continue her role as the attentive, eldest daughter—visiting Mother often, bringing her fruit, flowers, or the local weekly newspaper, or taking her a cup of tea in the afternoon.

Despite their long term companionship, Ann and Mother exchanged virtually no physical contact. In the past, each told me, in separate conversations, that they never touched, or hugged. I do recall, however, that on one occasion during the previous year, when Mother was feeling particularly weak, she asked Ann for assistance to climb the stairs to the bathroom. As they climbed, with Ann physically supporting Mother from the rear, Mother became incontinent, urine streaming down her legs and on to the stair carpet. As I heard the story from Ann, Mother felt humiliated, and Ann found that being responsible for Mother's physical safety was too overwhelming—and cleaning up the stair carpet was abhorrent to her.

That experience reinforced Ann's fear of taking additional responsibility for Mother's physical care and safety. Her horror of being unable to be there if needed, was rooted in there being no forewarning of a panic attack, which, when one occurred, kept her confined to her home, recuperating for several days.

Kevin was happy to do the grocery shopping during our stay at Mother's home, and on several occasions he gladly made delicious meals for us. During his visits to her room, he entertained Mother with his latest theories, stories of his latest inventions, and the patents he filed in Spain; or by pointing out the changes in the village, made evident to him by his examination of the pictorial history book. His presence was a great support and comfort to me—despite the some-what cramped quarters we shared, and my unfailing resistance to the constant flow of topics in which I held little interest.

Though I often find Kevin's manner exasperating, not because of who he is, but because of who I am—especially when he addresses me as the perpetual student to his uninvited teaching—I recognize with gratitude that to be with Mother at this critical time, he abandoned his income without a second thought. Mother often mentioned the pleasure Kevin's presence gave her, and I particularly appreciated his acts of great generosity and kindness while we were together.

Damian had not arrived as yet.

◆   ◆   ◆

17th June
6:45 PM

Hi my Love,

As I write, I picture you on your flight to the Cape.

Today, I backed five horses in five races. One won, one came in second, and I came out 20p ahead for the day. A lovely racing stable in Ireland, called Bally Doyle, was televised this afternoon. The countryside was exquisite. They didn't give the exact whereabouts, but the Bally Doyle area is certainly worth finding, just to be awash in a sea of emerald, and shelter from the rain with you, under the shade of tall, wind-swept, canopied trees.

Kevin has been reading all day. My mind has decided it is his coping mechanism, but what does my mind know?

Ann came to do her laundry and visited Mother for two hours.

Mother slept this evening, until the phone rang a minute ago—I think it is Damian. He's stopped calling at the requested hour. Damian's son, Phil, called the other day. Mother was happy to hear from him—another grandchild with whom she now has closure.

In the doctor's absence, his locum came: a rather large woman, wearing a calf-length, brown, tweed skirt, white blouse, and an open, button-to-the-neck, wooly cardigan. She put her briefcase on the bedroom chair and opened it; however, it was upside down, and scores of pills in sachets, syringes, and bits of paper, flew all over the floor, and she pothered about saying, "I've done this each time

I've opened it, today," and became even more agitated as she gathered everything up and flung it back into the briefcase, all higgledy-piggledy.

She checked Mother's pulse—and nothing else! I mentioned (out of Mother's earshot) that there was blood in Mother's urine on Sunday, but none since, and she said if it shows up again take a sample, and they'll check it. That's it! She'll be in again next week! A cursory visit indeed!

Today seems very long—partly because I know I can't reach you until tomorrow, and partly because there's no opportunity for me to actually go anywhere, besides the village. I'd like take a bus to the town, and to the hotel home of my childhood—the latter is now condominiums! It is just thirty minutes away. I'd love to see my old friend, dear Eunice T. But commodes, pills and comestibles come at too regular intervals for anything like that to occur. I think I'm feeling sorry for myself again—unbelievable how the mind churns out such self-inflicted pain! And that's what is.

8:00 PM

Since starting this letter, Mother has cleaned her teeth and finished her evening ablutions. I've changed her pad, and she is tucked up again. Damian and Norah have both phoned already, though the earlier call was not Damian after all, but a fellow-parishioner, who called Mother last week also. Norah talked with me, and asked if I would, "Please take a photo of Kevin with Enid," as she and Isabel (her twin) want one. "We haven't got *one* of them together," she lamented.

Kevin and Mother are both willing, so the plan is to take a photo or two tomorrow morning, Mother in her robe, hair coiffed, sitting in her commode chair, and Kevin sitting beside her, with flowers as a back drop. I notice how we all assume Mother will still be with us in the morning. It is remarkably unconscious to continue a lifetime's routine-expectation that Mother will always be here.

I've rearranged, into separate vases, what's left of the flowers that came from my children's father. They look even lovelier now, and Mother's room is redolent of the flower tent at the Royal Bath & West Show. She is pretty breathless tonight, but as she says, "... no pain." What with my comings and goings, and those of Kevin, Ann, Rachel, and the locum, she didn't have much rest today. Perhaps she'll sleep well tonight.

I called Eleanor and Barbara, they were out. Your brother-in-law Norman answered. I asked if Lucie's cremation had taken place, and he said, "I think so, but I'm not sure," which seemed rather odd, but I didn't pursue it.

Well love, the sun is going down behind the tall evergreens at the top of the street. The evening is setting in, and I think I'll have a beer and a piece of toast. I haven't eaten much today—no appetite.

I love you, talk soon,
Ju

P.S. I called the office to update my manager; I left her a voice-mail.

◆   ◆   ◆

18th June

Dearest HB,

How utterly privileged we are to be able to do what we are doing—you are on the Cape with all your kids, to attend the Memorial Service for Lucie, and I am here, not losing my job, caring for Mother.

Though I'm fully aware that all is in divine right order, I'm noticing that I'm feeling deeply disappointed about missing my kid's reunion.

I know how hard you've worked at the Sanctuary since I left, getting chores done, both for us, and for my children's arrival. The tipi pad you are putting in will be much easier to install using a power tamper with some strong young muscles shoveling the dirt. I do hope you'll ask my sons to help you with it. Jordan will probably want to help, he's very strong. I wonder if you got the paint and rollers for everyone to use, for his or her handprints—personalizing the tipi that way is such a good idea. So many things you planned to get finished. Be at peace with what is, my love. That's a reminder to me, as much as you.

I hope you can relax when my children arrive, and let them take care of the cooking and cleaning up. I know you'll need to get some space, and trust you will take care of yourself that way.

I stayed in last night, except for a brief trip to the Post Office at 8:30 to stretch my legs, and to catch today's first post. I finished reading the *Stieglitz and O'Keeffe* biography, by Benita Eisler—it's definitely the best I've read about Georgia's life. Thanks again for it. It depicts both characters as one-offs, selfish—in terms of excluding others to get their needs met—obsessive, avant-garde, and utterly dedicated to their art. I found them both absorbing and human, and she even more fascinating than he. Both enjoyed numerous other loves, all sexual;

his, always with young women; hers, with both men and women. You may enjoy reading about them; I'll bring it home.

Love, I want you to know that though a sense of place, and our Sanctuary, is important to me, it is not as important, or ever will be, as being with you, wherever. As much as I love where we live today, I think I can let it go. No place will ever claim me for good, only our love does that. So, selling up and traveling about, and may be having a condo as a base, in one of the western states, (I heard you say, preferably Arizona) would be fine. Despite the fact that my flexibility, contradicted by my attachment to our Sanctuary, seems somewhat daunting and unsettling to you, I want you to be happy, as happy as I am with you, wherever you want to go, whatever you want to do. I never cease to be in awe of the infinite love I feel for you and us. I dwell in love with you. It fills me up. You fill me up. We fill me up.

Kisses, love always, be well, talk with you soon,
Ju

Later
2:00 PM

Hi again.

Ascot races start in half an hour and I've placed four bets. One for each of the four races to be televised.

On the way to the betting shop, I stopped at Ann's for a short visit then went on to browse the market, picking up some fresh, locally-grown strawberries, and three Spanish peaches. We ate a small mound of Portobello mushrooms for lunch, cooked in a quarter pound of butter with scads of crushed garlic cloves, and served on toast. Delicious! Mother loved them.

I've not prepared the same daily menu since I arrived, so variety is the name of the game, though I'm not so sure about the balance I'm providing. I vary the vegetables, and prepare the chicken, or fish, differently each time. Some days Kevin and Mother have ham, or a hearty soup, or salmon.

Mother's doing well enough on it, she weighed ninety-four pounds when I arrived and—according to Gwen—still weighs the same now, despite fifteen days confined to bed. I imagine the tumor weighs grossly; it's growing, visibly. The doctor says Mother can eat and drink anything she likes. What difference does a "healthy" diet make at this point?

As I write, the TV is showing the Royal Party arriving at the Royal Ascot race course from Windsor Castle. They are in a coach and four—with white horses escorting front and rear—the outriders are in scarlet with black hats. Such a cavalcade! The first carriage has Queen Elizabeth, Prince Philip, Prince Charles, and a guest; the second, the Queen Mother, Princess Margaret, and two guests; the third, Princess Alexandria and a Lady Someone, and the fourth, Lady Emma and Lady Brook, with two young men. I don't recognize the latter. Someone's royal children I imagine.

The Queen's carriage horses, and those escorting, are all white. All others are chestnut, or brown. It is quite the English spectacle—and this, while there are homeless people in the streets of most major cities, and no doubt some are begging near the gates of the race course. And my mother is living with dying upstairs! Oh, the cognitive dissonance of it all!

The fashions are very colorful and must have cost a mint. Now, the Blues and Royals Band are striking up *God Save the Queen*, and the crowds are waving and cheering. It's a good thing it's not raining. The coachmen, looking very posh in their livery, doff their hats as the anthem plays. Then three "hip-hip-hoorays" rise up from the crowd, like the Who's of Whoville! All the men in sight have top hats—gray, or black—and colorful ties and 'weskits'. No cravats to be seen. Bring on the horses, I say!

I've placed a bet on the Queen Mother's horse in the second race—Daunting Lady—it seems appropriate. (It came in third!)

2:30 PM

Kevin is napping; a book dropped open in his lap; Mother's asleep, and I'm awake with you, and racing is on. It is a grand way to enjoy a Wednesday afternoon.

6:00 PM

Another horse I bet on came in fourth, (which paid winnings) and also a third. I lost a fiver—a small price for a fine afternoon of entertainment.

Mother has finished supper; she enjoyed soft cod roes on toast, and strawberries sprinkled with brown sugar. Ann came at 4:00, and visited Mother for two hours; she's just left.

Kevin kindly made supper—toasted crumpets drizzled with butter. I'm grateful for everything he does to help.

7:00 PM

Mother has just taken her seven o'clock medication. At 8:00, she and I will watch *A Touch of Frost,* a repeat of one I've seen, but new to Mother. I tried calling you at Eleanor's, but no reply, so I'm adding to this, just to be with you for a few extra minutes.

10:30 PM

It seems I'd only seen the last half of the *Frost* program and didn't remember the ending, so enjoyed it afresh, while Mother snoozed on and off, throughout.

She was very shaky on her legs tonight. I feel such deep, deep compassion for her. There's an odor about her now, despite the top-to-toe bathing each day. We are all very thorough, with effective clean-up after each bathroom break, and washing everything down with Dettol—that distinctive-smelling disinfectant that Mother has always used. We keep all the skylights open all day, and well into the evening. Mother resents the odor; she's always been so fastidious.

From a sitting position on the side of her bed, she now needs to be lifted from behind the knees and round her back, when I can swing her into position on to her pillows. She's unable to help at all. The medication has caused more blotches to appear on her legs and arms, which she avoids looking at. Nonetheless, her spirit is still cheerful, and she eats well, and rests pain-free between attentions from me, or visiting family, and caregivers.

I'll get this in the post in the morning.

I love you,
Ju

P.S. It began to rain at 10:40 PM—and is still raining at 6:00 AM.

◆   ◆   ◆

19th June
10:50 AM

Dearest HB,

Another letter came from you this morning. I felt deeply touched and moved to know that Barbara is singing solo at Lucie's service; so courageous of her.

I woke at first light, 4:00 AM, and switched on the BBC World Service, drifting in and out of sleep for a while. After a quiet visit to the bathroom I listened for Mother's breathing and could hear her, deep in slumber. Then I misread my watch and woke her at 6:00 AM. She was sound asleep when I went in—zzzz'ing away, which should have been a clue, but I was oblivious to clues. Kevin was snoring on the sofa downstairs, and my mind convinced itself that they were both oversleeping. I even concocted that it was because it piddled with rain all night—though why that should be, I don't know. My mind has a way of filling in any gaps of information.

Some of the grocery shopping is now done. Yesterday's letter is already posted to you, and I'm back here, making coffee for Rachel and Mother. Then, I'm off again, to Tesco's this time, to get fresh plaice to grill. Mother requested it.

And now I've returned and am making a coffee for Gwen, the R.N., who arrived while I was out. Kevin is going out shortly and I shall call you from here.

As you asked for details, here's an update on my health. After I'd been here for about a week, I woke up one morning with that same old pain in my groin—like the one that used to plague me during some of our visits here, and when we lived in California. Do you remember when I had to bend down and up, like a folding and unfolding ruler, and had to keep lifting my legs up and down, trying to ease out the discomfort? That was the time when Mother, Ann, you and I, went to Stoke Gabriel for the first time, and I concluded then that it was the cold, or humidity. You kindly drove all over Devon (slight exaggeration there) to find some zinc tablets. I remembered that occasion, and picked up some zinc from Holland and Barrett, and it did the trick again. What a relief! I'm remembering to take calcium, and as it's not possible to get dairy-free calcium tablets in the village, I'll count up what I have left and judge whether they will be enough. I'll let you know if I need any more.

Your letters are so comforting; when one arrives I scuttle off to 'my' bedroom and sit on the bed behind a closed door, just to have some space, and to be with you. I think this separation will be the longest we've had, even longer than when I lived in Geneva alone for a couple of months—before you joined me. It's a blessing that I'm so completely invested in caring for Mother, time does not drag at all. The days just feel very long, for which, in some ways, I'm truly thankful and in others not. That cognitive dissonance again!

11:00 AM

Ann has finished reading the latest Joanna Trollope book and is bringing it round for Mother to read.

The R.N. has left, and says they won't catheterize Mother unless she requests it, as the physical intrusion can cause infection. The alternative is larger pads: more absorbent, stay-dry-next-to-the-skin.

Mother seems to be even weaker today, and more unstable on her feet, but she managed to lock her knees when I lifted her on and off the commode. Care-giving to Mother is easy. She *never* complains and is cheerful, and accepting. I witness her deep serenity and grace, and I sense that this agreement between us was made in some prior lifetime—to be in support of her dying in her own home, in the most peaceful, and painless way possible.

I'm stopping now, to get lunch.

Lunch is over and it is still raining. Off to post this and to call you from the village, as there is no privacy here after all.

Kisses, and hugs, at 12:40 PM. I love you,
Ju

◆　　　◆　　　◆

My reference in the previous letter to care-giving being easy seems somewhat casual, though the ease of it has since given me cause to reflect.

Independently of one another, Hazel and Rachel often commented on Mother's grace and peacefulness in the face of death. Neither had experienced another client with the moment-to-moment serenity and acceptance that Mother demonstrated. Others who came to visit her were equally enchanted by her demeanor.

This was my first experience as a caregiver to a dying person, and to hear no complaining from my mother, about her condition and circumstances, filled me with wonder. She offered only questions, usually about the welfare of others, or shared her thoughts and feelings about her experience of dying. Words are quite inadequate to convey the ease with which she approached death. That's what made caring for her so easy. I felt blessed to witness her *being*, and being part of her process was an honor. She made it simple for me to remain alert to every nuance of her voice, facial expression, and physical movement—to any new signal that might indicate she needed something different from the care she was receiving. She was content with everything, except the odor about her, and the occasional irritation about the length of time it was taking her body to die.

◆　　　◆　　　◆

Same day
8:50 PM

Dearest HB,

Right now, you're probably making your way to the train station on your way to pick up Betsy. You expect her train in at about 10:00. How supportive of your youngest child to fly in from Sydney, to honor her grandmother, and be with you for Lucie's service.

Ann and I went out to supper this evening, to spend my winnings from the three days racing at Ascot—£26.27. The fourth race horse won at odds of 13–2. You won £10! I placed £1 each-way for you, on the favorite, Royal Applause. It was an utterly *fantastic* race. My horse came in second, Blue Goblin.

The new owners of #1 in the main house, an elderly couple, came into the pub while Ann and I were spending my winnings. They recognized Ann, and came over and kissed her hello. I felt so saddened to hear the woman say, as an aside to Ann that he, aged eighty-four, has cancer of the bowel, and she, aged seventy-five is "*petrified.*" My heart goes out to them both.

When Ann and I arrived back at 7:55—in time for me to wheel Mother to the bathroom to wash, clean teeth, eliminate, and change pad and panties—Damian called, and Mother relayed a message to me, to "Please book a room for the night of the 27th." It may be impossible to find him a room in his usual haunts; the village is so crowded and the local accommodations must surely be booked up.

Music on the Green, the huge, local festival, takes place on the 27th and 28th, and according to the local paper there are weddings galore this month. I'll have to try and book him in to some other place, perhaps in an adjacent hamlet.

Kevin is downstairs watching opera—he will most likely repeat his past behavior and criticize the pronunciation of the language in which they're singing. He does this regularly during TV programs, just as he criticizes the grammar when he reads anything. Now, am I observing or judging here? Yes, I'm judging! Just stop and move on, Judith. (This vignette reminds me of the times when I dissected every TV program and TV ad for my children, pointing out to them the sexism, ageism, racism and any other ism I was becoming familiar with when they were young! It must have driven them crazy!)

Mother is listening to the soundtrack of *Shine,* using the Walkman, another gift from Ann. She appears to be engrossed in the music, a quiet smile playing across her face, and her fingers are tapping a rhythm on her bed cover. I'll find out what she thought of it when I go back in for the next bathroom break, and the last medication of the day. (She "… loved it!")

By the time you actually receive this, my kids will have begun to arrive at our Sanctuary, or their arrival is imminent. While they are there, please take very good care of you in every way. Write to me every day please, if you have time, and fill me in on the comings, goings, doings, beings, and conversations that you are a part of, and take lots of pictures, please. With your help, I intend to participate vicariously in my children's reunion, even if at a later date!

Tonight, Mother could not stand—and said so—she could hardly see the TV screen this afternoon. She's worse than yesterday. Her body is weaker and her spirit is slowly marshalling the energy with which it will expel itself from her form. That makes sense to me somehow. By Monday, or before, she'll not be able to get out of bed at all.

HB, there are no words to express my appreciation for our life together. Or express how I appreciate you. Infinitely, doesn't come close. Words are so inadequate.

Kisses to you, I love you sweetheart, more in the morning,
Ju

Friday
10:00 AM

Mother, awake at 7:00, is cheerful, though very dizzy and wobbly. All care given as usual.

I'm waiting for Hazel to arrive to bathe her then I'll make them both coffee and go to Tesco's, to get a bottle of champagne. Kevin has finished the food shopping already. We are having another picnic in Mother's room to celebrate the last day of racing at Ascot.

When I was growing up, these special sports events were ones that our family often enjoyed together. And now, I'm so aware that we are sharing them together for the last time, and my mind wanders off, thinking they will be good memories for Mother—only to jolt back to reality.

Off to post this to you, my love. I trust Betsy, and your dear son, JR, have arrived safely. Talk with you in a couple of hours.

Later

The photos of the Sanctuary garden came today—how utterly superb they are. Thank you, my love. I feel the deepest peace, drinking in every petal and leaf; the textures; every light and shadow; every rock. How *gorgeous* everything looks. You are an angel. What an incredibly fortunate woman I am, to have you in my life.

Love,
Ju

◆   ◆   ◆

20th June
6:00 PM

Dearest HB,

I do apologize for ranting and raving, letting off steam today on our phone call, without giving you the slightest chance to tell me any of your news, other than JR's and Betsy's safe arrival at the airport. I'm glad you're all going down to the Cape, en caravan.

Today, it's been piddling down again, with one hour—between 4:30 and 5:30 PM—of blue sky and sunshine. People here complain about the rain—it must be a conditioned response. With an umbrella one doesn't get wet at all. I went out three times today, returning with dry clothes, each time.

There were six races televised from Ascot, you and I not a winner or place between us, (seven bets). You are now £8 ahead as I write, and I'm £2.27 ahead. Enough for a very light lunch for two, anywhere we like, when I get home.

For her supper this evening, Mother ate one and a half toasted tea-cakes, slathered with butter and blackcurrant jam; a pear, peeled and sectioned, and a glass of Fortimel—a fortified protein drink, which the doctor has now prescribed for her; she ate the lot with gusto.

Ann is now upstairs visiting. I'm off to the Globe Inn, to see if a double room has become available for Damian and TA for next Friday night.

I'll get back to this later.

7:30 PM

I enjoyed a half pint at the Globe but no room was available. So I came back and called Tony at our favorite B & B. How many times would you guess we've stayed there, a dozen perhaps, over the years? They have a room available. Hooray!

Tony sent his condolences and very best to you. He and Alison both have parent health-issues going on as well. They said it is difficult to run the business at the same time as giving care. I cannot imagine how they do that!

For supper, I made myself a sandwich, using a whole avocado, a little lettuce, and a fresh tomato; a cup of Good Earth tea rounded it off very nicely. Thank you again for the tea. You are with me in so many ways, my love.

Tonight, Mother is wondering, "What it will be like to ... just die," and I told her of things I've read, written by folk who had a near-death-experience, wherein they report going into a nurturing light, joy and peace filling their spirit; that their breath has behind it a gentle energy as the spirit is expelled into a blissful light.

Mother smiled sweetly to herself, and said softly, "I think it *is* that way—I can't imagine anything else."

I added, for what I hoped might be additional comfort, "I'll be here with you, to support you having a loving and peaceful transition."

She beamed up at me, "That's the *best* part. *You'll* be here with me!"

I left her and went to 'my' room and wept. I feel so honored; so joyful; so completely bereft.

Mother is much weaker today, despite her appetite. No! Not appetite. She says she doesn't have one anymore, but the food "... looks and tastes so delicious," she says, "I just can't help eating it all."

Despite her eating so well, she declines a little more every day, and loses a little more facility. Many more blotches have appeared on her legs, arms and hands.

The evening sun (7:50 now) is pouring its golden light into the sitting room, the patio door is ajar. I'm beguiled by a blackbird's rapturous evensong and it lifts my spirit like a windblown kite, giddy with delight. Kevin is watching the news and harrumphing. Such is the moment.

Earlier, rain was forecast for Saturday, Sunday, and Monday, clearing on Tuesday. When I went to Tesco's in the rain this morning, I stopped en route to look at the gardens in Market Street. The stillness, colors, and textures of the exquisite blooms filled me with a sense of peace and wonder. Another lovely moment, being present to the beauty of nature in the tender hands of devoted U.K. gardeners. I felt renewed!

I need to stop. It's time to administer to Mother—medication, elimination, wash, brush hair, clean teeth and partial plate, change pad and panties, and tuck up until 10:00 PM. Damian, Norah, and Isabel, are due to call soon. I'll write more in the morning.

21st June
Saturday
10:30 AM
Summer solstice

Up at 7:00 AM, and Mother is in high spirits, and strong voice.

Last night, just before sleeping, Mother listened to the first two parts of *The Shell Seekers,* by Rosamund Pilcher. She so enjoyed it, she is planning to listen to the third and fourth parts tonight. Over the years, Ann has bought Mother many books on tape, and now that she has taken her maiden flight on the Walkman, I think she'll enjoy them all. In the stack of tapes in her nightstand is one you sent her, *Joshua,* and some by Anne Tyler, and two or three more by Pilcher, and one by Dick Francis, so she's in for some lovely evenings of light entertainment—that is if she is here.

She could not stand again this morning, her legs just buckle. I know it can't be many days before she's confined solely to her bed—no commode, no wheeling, or dancing to the bathroom to our music of the moment, *In the Mood.* Though, today, Mother said, "Now, I'm looking forward to Damian arriving *and,* if I make it, the first anniversary of my surgery on 18th July!"

It's piddling down again, having started off sunny and bright. Kevin is watching a VW auto-racing program, taking place here in England. No cricket yet, due to rain; play stopped when England's score was 38 for 3—we are playing Australia for the Ashes, in another match of the series.

I'll be holding you in my heart all day, and I'll be at the Cathedral from 4:00 until 5:00, joining you, in spirit, at the time of Lucie's Memorial Service on the Cape. St. Cuthbert's bells have been peeling since 9:00 AM, and I've been imagining they're ringing for Lucie today, when all of us closest to her can rejoice in her life. I so appreciate her gift to the world of you, and her acceptance of me into her family.

Here's a short story: I did the laundry earlier, and Kevin, who arrived twelve days ago with one little grip bag for luggage, just now, said, "Do you think I should take my suit out of this bag?"

I offered that it might be a good idea and, from the bottom of the little bag, he lifted out his suit. It was partially shrouded in plastic, falling off its hanger, sporting very well-pressed creases—in all the wrong places.

It occurs to me that we'll be the oddest looking bunch at Mother's funeral. Damian will probably come in an open neck shirt, tracksuit pants, and flip-flops. This may sound very peculiar, but I thank Infinity that Mother won't be there, to see us seeing her off. She'd be mortified—though, on the other hand, I like to imagine she would try to conceal a smile, and the little dimple under her right eye would give it away, as she'd giggle to herself, thinking, "Oh, my irreverent children!"

Love and kisses,
Ju

◆   ◆   ◆

21st June
Early evening

Dearest HB,

Today was another emotional one in so many ways. Such deep sadness that Lucie has gone. I have so many memories of her kindnesses to me. In this moment, it is inconceivable that her physical presence is no longer on this earth.

I went to the Cathedral as planned, to join all of you at the Memorial Service on Cape Cod, mourning by myself, yet accompanied by a heavenly, boys' choir, practicing Evensong. I lit four candles, one for Lucie, one for Mother—to light her journey—one for us, and one for our families. It struck me as odd that I felt compelled to perform that ritual.

Ann brought me flowers as a condolence, and later, phoned to offer me support because, as she perceives it, I'm not with you on this difficult day. I appreciate her thoughtfulness—and I was with you.

Love you,
Ju

◆   ◆   ◆

21st June
10:30 PM

Hello my Love,

Just off the phone with you, the service for Lucie over—and your grieving has deepened in earnest. It is healing to grieve. Be with it, surrender to it.

I called Anna, briefly. She's looking forward to the reunion at our Sanctuary, though I could hear it is a slight effort for her to go, now that she knows I won't be there. And knowing Anna, she'll choose to enjoy it once she arrives.

It is weeping rain on the skylight, great sobbing drops, plinking down on the smooth cheek of the glass; just as mine flowed, freely and silently, in the Cathedral, today. I filled up with images of Lucie, in restaurants together; gardening with her, or for her; at Spruce Point in Booth Bay; in her home with you. She is loved and missed, and is now at peace with all the energies of her departed family and friends.

I need to sleep now. I'll add to this later.

◆   ◆   ◆

22nd June
Sunday
9:30 AM

At 7:00 this morning, Mother was shaking involuntarily from head-to-toe, ice-cold hands and face. I fetched a wool blanket, and a warm face cloth and towel, to freshen her face, eyes, and mouth, and patiently coaxed her to take the first two pills, which she downed with small sips of water.

She needed to urinate, and I gave her the choice—to fill the extra-absorbent pad she now wears, or try for the commode when she warmed up. She chose, "… the commode, when we can do it."

Twenty minutes later, she was warm, and lifting her took a lot of leveraging and supporting. She couldn't bear her own weight but put her feet on the floor, and with me turning us both, and pulling her pants-with-pad down with one hand, and literally holding her up against me with the other, we made it. She shook the entire time, and her lovely face held a pinched expression; her eyes, vacant.

I got her back into bed and she managed a cup of tea, which enabled her to swallow seven more of her pills, and she ate three small spoonfuls of apple sauce, with a chopped prune. This is her worst morning.

It's after breakfast now.

While I bathed, Mother slept then Kevin popped in to see her for five minutes; she soon told him she needed to sleep again.

Kevin seems nervous this morning, moving things from here to there then back again, and I'm breathing consciously, focusing in the present. It would be easy to get caught up in the resistance to losing her. I must stay in spirit and be here for her, in *her* world, for *her* needs, nowhere else. I'll call you at 2:15 today.

I love you,
Ju

10:05 AM

Mother's particularly thirsty, so I'm in 'my' room writing this, listening for her voice, "May I have some more water, please," she calls out, every five minutes or so. She can't reach for or hold a glass by herself. Hazel is due in to bathe her, and someone from the church, to give her Communion.

The current challenge is to release any expectation that what Mother could do yesterday, she can do today. Or even an hour ago!

Mother said to be sure to tell you, "Judith is an angel," and that she can almost see my wings, and "… how very, very much …" your support for me being here, "… is appreciated." She is the angel of course.

I'll end here, more, later. I love you, sweetheart,

Kisses,
Ju

◆   ◆   ◆

22nd June
1:15 PM

Dearest HB,

Kevin told me of a book fair being held at the Town Hall, today. He spied some Henry Williamson books in the racks. So he spelled me, and I took twenty-five minutes away, and found two books I think you'll enjoy. You may have one of them already, *The Dark Lantern*. I bought it anyway. It is the first in the series: *A Chronicle of Ancient Sunlight* and another, not part of the series, *Life in a Devon Village*. I've started reading the latter. It is appealing in the way only Williamson can offer.

Vincent is on holiday, in Cheltenham for the weekend, and Father Jim is no doubt glued to the TV show, the Simpson's—he confessed to being strongly addicted!—before he whisks himself away to another parishioner's home, for his Sunday lunch.

Thus, Dr. Trafford came to give Mother Communion. He is eighty-four, an ex-army officer, tall and slim, with grey eyes, rheumy with old age. On coming downstairs, he said of Mother, "She's so serene, so peaceful." And he smiled, murmuring to himself as he left, "Wonderful, wonderful!"

The fare for lunch is a delicious, light soup, and roasted breast of chicken. Mother ate so little at breakfast I thought it might be easier for her to have something light. The doctor says she can eat anything she feels like, and she may also continue to imbibe her favorite red wine, Beaujolais Village, of which she has a little every day—one glass before lunch, one with lunch, and perhaps another in the early evening. I'm happy to oblige.

I served her a small bowl of soup, with finely chopped chicken breast and two "soldiers" of buttered bread (a term left-over from our childhood, for what are now referred to as "fingers"). She took three sips of soup and two bites of one soldier, before saying, "That's enough," and her eyes closed, her breathing, more shallow. As I took her tray and began to leave her room, she called, "Thank you for not making me eat it all," and then continued in almost a whisper. "I don't feel as though I'm all here today. The room is fading!"

I put down the tray and returned to her bedside. Taking her hand, I asked softly, "Is the room fading because you aren't seeing so well now, or is it something else?"

"Oh, it's something else. Not the same at all."

"Are you preparing to leave?"

"Perhaps," she replied.

Then, she added, "That's what's so puzzling, not knowing what it will be like, but then, no one knows, do they?"

"I've only heard that the moment is peaceful, when one has no resistance to it."

"That's good," she said, and closed her eyes to sleep.

Just prior to this conversation, Kevin put his head round her bedroom door, to say, "God bless, Ma," then he added, "Good-bye, Ma."

When I went down for my writing paper, Kevin said, "She doesn't have long does she?" It came more as a statement.

I asked him, "If I'm with her and realize that she's leaving imminently, do you want me to call you, to be with her?"

"Uh, let's play that by ear, shall we?"

"Whatever your decision, she will understand." Then more to myself, I added, "Maybe she'll choose to go alone, without any of us." (Though in retrospect, I know that's not so.)

He said nothing. I sense he's quietly on edge. A little later he said, "By the look of it I'll be able to catch my return flight after all." His return reservation is booked for 4th July.

I ate a good lunch, my appetite unimpaired today.

I'm signing off for a bit now. Rain is piddling down onto the always-open skylight above my head. The room is fresh and cool.

Back soon, love. I am present in this moment, knowing I'll talk with you by phone, as planned, in thirty-five minutes.

6:45 PM

So good to talk with you and feel your support. I think I'm going to be weepy on and off, oozing tears in a phone booth—reminiscent of the drip system in our courtyard.

Quite oddly, it feels somewhat comforting that our mothers are going back-to-back, only because we can understand each other's feelings, and can truly empathize. Thank you for being there. In this house, there is no acceptance of any outward expression of grief. Stoicism is all we were ever taught, and cajoled to show. The stiff-upper-lip syndrome is such an ingrained part of the English character, and our family culture.

I relayed your message to Enid, "HB says to tell you he loves you," and with her eyes closed, she smiled gently, and whispered, "And I love him."

"He knows," I responded, giving her hand a gentle squeeze.

Her expression softened, emotion showing on her face. She absorbed your love.

Ann came in for a while, visiting with Mother for forty-five minutes. While she was still here, I carried up a tray with Mother's supper—a sliver of fresh, hot, apple and blackberry pie, and half a small carton of yogurt. She downed the lot.

I talked with Anna last night. She asked me to ask Mother to, "Stop by ..." (wherever Anna is at the time) "... on her journey to the next level."

She also encouraged me again to be present moment-to-moment. I need the reminder and appreciate hearing it. Anna is so supportive. I feel blessed to have you both supporting me ... oh, it is 7:00 PM; pill time; I must leave you for a bit.

7:45 PM

I just managed to get Mother on the commode without dropping her. She's bleeding again. I've taken a sample and have it ready for the R.N. to take when she comes in tomorrow. Mother managed to swallow her pills, and wash her hands, face, and neck. I cleaned her partial plate, and gently brushed her hair.

She's sleeping peacefully now, and will probably do so until 8:00, when more pills are due. When I gave Mother Anna's message—about stopping by—she responded very readily that she will be happy to visit her en route.

She wants to watch the fourth installment of *Jewel in the Crown* from 9 to 10 tonight, though she can't actually see the screen clearly any more. May be it's a way for her to stay in touch with the familiar.

When I peeped in at 7:00 PM, she was deeply asleep, but the floor board creaked, and she woke with a start. Looking up beyond the skylight, she said with great surprise, "Oh, it's a bright sunny day, and you are all dressed! You're even wearing earrings! What time is it? Did I oversleep?"

I love the long, light, summer evenings here.

I love you sweetheart, kisses,

Ju

◆   ◆   ◆

23rd June
10:40 AM

Hi Love,

Mother is in better shape than yesterday. She fed herself two prunes and a spoonful of apple sauce, downed three soldiers of toast, and drank two cups of tea. Pretty good, I thought. She has more strength than yesterday, and is most cheerful.

Hazel has arrived, and Kevin has returned from the shops. Now I'm in 'my' room with the door closed, taking a bit of space.

It is amazing to observe the ego popping up, again, and again. I realize that I felt sorry for myself again yesterday. Unbelievable! There is such infinite peace when I stay present with an open heart, and attach no importance to what my mind is thinking, or to what my ego wants.

Last night I got up several times, to check on Mother's warmth and breathing; she slept soundly until 7:00 AM.

Ann came in and invited me to supper tonight.

Your letter came, written en route to Cape Cod, and added to on Thursday as you left to pick up Betsy. Your worries about JR not making it to the Memorial Service were happily unfounded.

Sorry to have disturbed your rest when I called last night. I know how much you need those breaks, and space, especially when with a crowd—even a loved crowd.

I'm going to make coffee for Hazel, Mother and Kevin; then I'll get this off in the post to you before lunch. I'm making a lentil roast, with French fries, and apple and blackberry pie, topped with yogurt. Perhaps Mother will be able to eat some. Must go!

I love you, more later,
Ju

Same day
4:10 PM
Cricket and Wimbledon are being televised

Hi Love,

You sounded tired when we talked today, and tomorrow you fly home, in time to welcome my children to our Sanctuary.

The R.N., Gwen, came in this afternoon. I gave her the sample of blood taken yesterday. She brought with her a V-shaped pillow intended to support Mother sitting up more comfortably. Mother delighted in using it right away. It's soft, yet firm. Gwen also brought a nylon easy-glide sheet. It is intended to facilitate maneuvering a patient in and out of bed, but the instructions are for two caregivers working with a patient in a single bed. So if it isn't really helpful, I'll return it. Using it is supposed to reduce the likelihood of caregivers getting a back strain, and to avoid friction, from the sheets, on Mother's pressure points. I feel blessed and grateful for the availability of all these helpful items.

The lentil roast was met with utter disdain by everyone. A culinary failure!

This afternoon Mother slept for two and a half hours, and after her three o'clock pills, a commode break, and a cup of lemon tea, she snoozed right off again.

Ann stopped in, on her way to the shops. She's coming back to visit Mother before she and I have supper out tonight. Kevin will be here while we're out.

Mother confided that she's more and more curious about what death is like, but said, "You know, Judith, this may seem a funny thing to say in the circumstances, but right now I'm *completely* happy and content. It's wonderful to be so pampered and coddled. I'm even happier than when we lived in Ryton. I thought those were the happiest days of my life, but *these* are."

Today, the sun shone, and white clouds billowed in the bluest sky—a pretty spring day in the middle of summertime; it warmed up a bit, and may even have reached 60°F.

5:30 PM.

I've just served Mother's supper, a glass of Fortimel and a huge piece of chocolate fudge cake that Ann bought for her. According to Ann, Mother loves this particular type of cake, and when Mother saw it on the tray her eyes lit up, like a child seeing her first snow fall.

6:00 PM

I miss talking with you, in person, miss knowing I can reach you easily, miss our lunches out, miss our breakfasts and suppers together; miss being at home with you, hanging out; miss being with you, miss our togetherness; miss our early mornings in bed; miss listening to National Public Radio with you; miss watching *As Time goes By* with you. I'm surrounded by so many people, yet I feel so utterly alone, as perhaps each one of us does here. Uh, oh! Here I am, feeling sorry for myself *again*. And surrender to that too, Judith! So be it.

10:15 PM

At 6:05, Ann and I left for the City Arms—Kevin was more than willing to give Mother her seven o'clock pills that I put out for her—and at 7:30, who jaunts into the pub, but a beaming Damian, his thinning hair sun-bleached, and his blue-green eyes holding their ever-present twinkle. He was sucking on a Gauloise cigarette, and dressed in his favorite attire: tracksuit pants, tee shirt and flip flops. He's four days earlier than expected!

Ann and I were utterly delighted to see him. Mother's first born, here at last. He said that when I told him, last night on the phone, that Mother had a bad day, he'd heard my deeper meaning. He took a flight from Geneva at 10:00 AM this morning, then a bus from Heathrow, and another to here, and came straight to the pub. He said he needed a drink after the journey and hurried to the bar, standing tall as he waited to be served, his back held ramrod straight, as usual. He ordered a Guinness and a Somerset smoky: smoked haddock, with creamed-spinach sauce, and mashed potatoes topped with melted cheese—served in a ramekin.

When I finished my smoked salmon, I left for the Globe Inn to see if they had a single room through Thursday night. They did, in the attic. I booked it, then quickly returned to Mother's, administered her eight o'clock pills, washed her face, brushed her hair and, while I cleaned her partial plate, she brushed her teeth. I said not a word about Damian being here, and just spruced her up, knowing she'd want to look her very best for him.

Damian walked into her bedroom at 8:30. When he said "Hello there," in his deep, warm, voice, she didn't recognize it at first, and couldn't see him clearly enough to know him as he walked in. Then the penny dropped, and she cried out with such love and delight, "Damian," and blushed with pleasure, which was quickly followed by her best hospitality voice, asking, "What can we get you to drink?" And as he leaned over to kiss her she reached for his hand, pulled him down, and kissed his cheeks several times, with such vigor and joy.

Damian brought with him a large bottle of Irish whiskey, and helped himself to a tot, and Mother requested, "… a third of a glass of red wine, please, Judith, to celebrate!" After filling her request, I left them alone; Mother's joy, palpable.

Damian came downstairs at 9:45, in time to hear Kevin express righteous indignation at a TV program, which was recounting the sexual antics of British politicians in the late 1950's. I went upstairs and Mother was so very, very happy, "Damian's here. I can't believe it." The glow on her face was beautiful.

She used the commode, took her last pills at 10:00, and is now in the land of nod, which is where I'm going, shortly.

I've closed my bedroom door to keep the smoke out from the black tobacco cigarettes that Damian smokes. After he leaves for the Globe and the air clears, I'll open up, so I can hear Mother in the night.

I thought of you in Nashua, shopping for something you couldn't resist at L. L. Beans. Talk with you tomorrow.

I love you, HB,
Ju

◆   ◆   ◆

24th June
Tuesday
6:30 AM

I woke up earlier than usual and listened to the *Farming News* on BBC 4. There was an argument going on, about whether British Farmers should "grow more lamb" in the autumn, to meet the British Public's increased demand for more lamb between January and June. "Impossible," says the British Farmers' spokesperson, "It will just bring prices down. We can't have that!" Then *Prayer for the Day* came on at 6:26 AM, so I switched off and here I am, switched on to you.

9:20 AM

The morning routine is completed, plus deadheading the flowers, and changing their water, which they need each day. Keeping Mother's flowers fresh, clean, and lovely, is part of the nurturing.

In the post today, Mother received a lovely card from the son of a dearly loved, late friend from the parish. The son is the artist who painted the beautifully sensitive water color of the cathedral; you may remember it; it hangs in Mother's hallway. Mother bought it from him many years ago. To receive a card from him meant a great deal to her. The subject of the card is a delicate water color of three vases of flowers, by Auguste Rodin, and is elegantly lovely. Mother's voice and expression softened as she read his words, and tears welled—more closure.

When I got up this morning I was in a foul mood. I thought at first it was due to the farming discussion, (envisioning little lambs gamboling over the fields, being grown for a Sunday roast), or perhaps not switching off the radio before having *Prayer for the Day* imposed. After some objective digging, I found the source. With Damian here, I'm aware of feeling even more hemmed-in, and know there's another mouth to feed.

When I realized that the self-generated feeling—expertly enabled by my chattering mind—of being taken for granted by yet one more person, I let it all go peacefully, and returned to the silence within. *No-one* takes me for granted here. So often I trap myself in my ego's automatic, pain-inducing, habitual thought patterns. I'm fine now. It had nothing to do with Damian being here, or anyone else, just my mind chattering on, and my ego, flexing again.

Today, we are having a picnic for five in Mother's bedroom, a family celebration, with smoked salmon and champagne. It will delight Mother, all of us together for a meal in her own home. It is a rare occasion. The last time was at my father's funeral, twenty-one years ago.

Damian's just arrived from the Globe Inn and is with Mother as I write.

The window cleaners have also arrived. As Mother explained to me, "They come once a month, on the last Tuesday, whether the windows need it or not." I quietly told the window cleaners that if no one is here next month, to just do the outside, and discreetly paid them for it in advance.

Ann talked last night about her growing realization that she will be very lonely when Mother dies. She will have no family member to talk with, in person, whenever she likes, and she hinted at her belief that our brothers, and perhaps even I, will not come to England to see her again. I could only say that I understood her anxiety and said no more, for now. This is such a challenging time for each of us, in different ways and for a myriad of reasons.

As I must get this to the post—much love, and kisses to you, HB,

Ju

◆   ◆   ◆

Still the 24th June
Tuesday
1:50 PM
In 'my' bedroom

Dearest HB,

It was so good to talk with you before you left for the airport with JR.

At the picnic all four siblings perched around the bed on dining chairs, or stools. Mother proposed a toast and, beaming with utter joy, she raised her glass; in unison we followed her lead and, looking from face to face, we toasted our reunion, "To being together." We sipped the champagne then quietly went about helping ourselves to the choices before us.

The picnic made an aesthetically-pleasing spread, so many vibrant colors and diverse textures; smoked salmon with lemon; stuffed green olives; asparagus tips; hot, new potatoes gleaming with melted butter; soldiers of buttered wholemeal bread, and quarters of hard boiled-eggs; we enjoyed sections of cantaloupe for dessert. As before, it was all served on Mother's *Belle Fiore* china and eaten with her silver fish knives and forks—resplendent on the linen cloth. It was all very festive.

Mother is so deeply under the influence of medication now, she's occasionally muddling up facts, people and places. I begged Ann to stop correcting her—only because I observe that, when corrected, Mother becomes *aware* that she's muddled, and gets very anxious. Ann agreed, and I'm sure she'll follow through. All of our family members have the verbal habit of correcting one another whenever we think some aired "fact" is just plain incorrect—and now is not the time to impose that habit on Mother.

Kevin has Damian cornered downstairs, (though I doubt that Damian feels that way) and is giving him a Spanish lesson! Damian has spoken the language for at least forty years longer than Kevin. Kevin is also inundating him with minutia about the pictorial history of the village, and what has and hasn't changed. Damian is such a good-hearted chap. He's generously paying attention, while downing doubles of whiskey. I think he'll leave soon to have a nap at the Globe, and Kevin usually sleeps after lunch. I'm noticing, as I write, how my irrational and habitual judgments just keep coming up.

Between trips upstairs to care for Mother I hoped to watch some play at Wimbledon for an hour; however, with Damian and Kevin chatting downstairs, and the washing machine droning on with the daily changes of linen, nightgowns, panties and socks, I don't think the TV will be particularly audible. So instead, I'm here with you. A fine trade!

It is 9:50 AM, EDT, where you are, and you are probably taxiing down the runway, or already in the air, so safe journey home, my love. I cannot imagine my life without you—long may such devastation of the heart be postponed.

3:45 PM

Mother has taken her 3:00 PM medication.

Just prior to that, at about 2:40, and 2:45, and again at 2:50, the phone rang, and each time I heard an intermittent signal, beep … beep … beep … beep … beep … beep, until I hung up. I decided it was you calling me from the air, at least in your thoughts, if not in reality. The egocentricity of my mind!

Right now, Boris Becker is serving to a chap named Gorriz. Becker is almost through to the next round. Tim Henman (GBR) got through to the second round. Vicario-Sanchez and Hingis are both through to the next round. Perhaps you'll watch Wimbledon with David, when he and my other kids arrive at our Sanctuary. It may still be on.

Damian eventually left for the Globe to sleep. Kevin is still asleep on the sofa. Mother slept from 1:00 to 3:00 PM, and I'm making merry with some personal space.

Here's an example of Mother's growing confusion. She says she has forgotten the floor plan of her home and cannot remember what the house looks like from the outside. She commented, "But I'd rather have no memory than pain!"

Continuing on the 25th June
Wednesday, 9:30 AM

Now I know, for sure, that I won't be with you all on 4th July. Now that it is definite, I experience such cognitive dissonance about it: on the one hand, I'm sorry to miss the pure enjoyment of sharing our Sanctuary with my children and you, and, on the other, I feel so privileged to be here, in service to Mother.

Last week, while cleaning the bathroom, I reorganized it, quite unconsciously, by moving all of Mother's personal things to one side, just to make it easier for me to empty and disinfect the commode pan. This morning I noticed, as I put Mother's things back in their former place, how making these small changes affect the perspective of her "staying" or "leaving." It was an arresting moment; to reflect what is, I moved all her things aside again.

Being present to each moment helps me to stay in touch with the reality of her dying. She looks so young, for all her eighty-four years. Absolutely not one line is visible in her face, as the medication has plumped her cheeks out, round and smooth. (I wonder if the medication contains any of what chickens are fed, to make them look plump for the supermarket. This is just a connecting thought—the mad mind at work again!)

I brush Mother's hair several times a day, just to nurture and comfort her. She moisturizes her face with Olay after I wash her each morning, and I dab Chanel #5 on her pulse points. So, from the shoulders up, in a very pretty nightgown, she looks absolutely wonderful. It's very easy for anyone, who doesn't give personal care to her body below her shoulders, to hold on to the illusion of normalcy.

Wendy, the auxiliary nurse, is here now, bathing Mother from the shoulders down. A moment ago, I stopped writing to take Wendy some cookies and an orange juice, and to make Mother a coffee. The entire time she's working on Mother, Wendy chit-chats about this and that, (like I do in these letters!) and Mother responds with brief comments like, "Really!" or, "Well, I never," or, "Would you believe it," while all the time her body is moved about, like a tender piece of meat at the butchers—but with rubber gloves, sponges, soaps and towels, instead of chopping blocks, cleavers, and bloody aprons.

Kevin is reading the newspaper downstairs and tells me that Compaq has bought Tandem for a $3 billion share swap. That's a nice deal for Tandem, their relatively new President worked very quickly.

Today, for lunch, we're having cold roast chicken, potato salad, fresh baby greens, and buttered new potatoes, with parsley.

Damian just came in, after enjoying a big breakfast at the Globe.

I've been thinking about your supportive offer to come over to join me. Frankly, with the full house here, I'd suggest that if you do decide to come, come just for the funeral, and stay until I leave, which will be approximately two weeks later. You could rent a car and we could fly back together. In the event that you feel you can't really face another long journey (so soon after flying to the east coast and back), I completely support that decision, and understand, with unconditional love.

I'm doing well today and feel strong enough to be with the emotional challenges.

Kisses, hugs, and love,
Ju

◆   ◆   ◆

25th June
10:45 PM
In 'my' bedroom

Dearest HB,

At 10:15 tonight, Mother finished listening to a three hour audio tape—*September*, by Rosamund Pilcher. I can't remember the gist of the story, but it seemed to affect Mother in a way I don't understand. When I lifted her gently onto the commode, she said, *so* self-critically, "I'm such a *pest*, Judith!"

My retort was the same as on the few previous occasions when she's said these same exact words. "I thought we'd agreed to give up this particular conversation. You're not a pest at all."

Then she began to weep, and said, "I don't want to leave you."

With my heart breaking and tears welling, I put my arms round her, saying, "Why don't you want to leave?"

"Because we are so happy together," her voice, so filled with anguish.

I just held her hand as she tried valiantly to swallow back her tears; I suggested that it is really good to cry.

"I'm alright. I'm alright," she said, trying to convince herself, and perhaps me. Her body was convulsed with sobs.

I searched for words of comfort but none came. She continued to weep.

Such was her effort to hold back the tears she couldn't urinate, and asked to be put back into bed. She swallowed the last pills of the day and, when I lay her down, I asked if she'd like to talk some more.

"I'd better not. I'll only cry some more and I don't want to cry, it puts *you* in such a terrible position."

"Let's talk anyway," I said, gently taking her hand again.

I put her tissues within easy reach and shared with her that there is *nothing* I would prefer to be doing now. I told her that supporting her is the highest privilege, and I believe it is our karma to be here now, experiencing her dying process, together. I told her that I believe she gave birth to me to support me learning, understanding, and fulfilling the intention of our relationship. And this is it.

"Yes, it is our karma, isn't it?" She said. Then added softly, "Go to bed now Judith, I'm alright." She kissed my hand, and tears puddled at the outer corners of her eyes and then trickled slowly down each side of her face, through her soft, baby-fine hair and onto the pillow, creating small, damp circles of grief. She clung to me for a moment longer, and whispered, "Goodnight, dear."

I whispered softly, "Mother, you know that I love you and want to be here, no matter how long it takes. I know you are deeply happy with all of us here now, and with me caring for you. I know you love us all. When you are ready, it will be okay to go."

"I'm not hanging on!" she explained.

"I know."

She paused, then, "Thank you for everything, Judith."

"Goodnight, Mother. Damian and Kevin said goodnight, too."

"Goodnight Damian. Goodnight Kevin."

I kissed her and left her room.

While we were holding hands, tears streamed down my face; I said something to the effect that being present at a birth and a death are surely the most intimate events that can be experienced; she nodded her assent. I am so moved; this time with her is so cherished. Tomorrow, if she's here and remembers the conversation, she'll probably apologize. It would be so like her.

I wanted to call you to share this verbally. I'm so *full*. I need to release some of this emotional energy so I can sleep; there's no privacy to call you from here, so I've chosen to write it down, rather than find a vacant phone box in the village, especially at this time of night.

I love you, sweetheart. I'm so happy that you're back at our Sanctuary safely. Please do nothing to exacerbate your back pain.

By the time you read this, it will probably be the 3rd or 5th July, and all my children will be with you. When you all go to the local café, enjoy a glass of Pouilly Fuisse for me. It will be a fun time, and I'll join you, in spirit.

Damian says he and TA leave for Greece next Tuesday, on a charter flight from London. They are going on holiday. That's why they were coming here on the 27th, to see TA's family, and Mother. Then they'll be off. Damian asked me to book them into the B & B (where you and I have so often stayed), for Sunday, Monday and *Tuesday* nights. He'd momentarily forgotten they are planning to leave on Tuesday. I can only surmise how this is affecting him.

He has a very gentle demeanor when he's with Mother, speaking softly, listening attentively, hearing her words, and their meaning. They care so deeply for each other, evident in the tone and intimacy of their voices, which I can hear from 'my' room.

He and Kevin were startled by a sudden question from Mother, this evening. At her invitation the three of us were visiting her together, when she said, unconnected to anything that I could discern, "What would you boys do if I popped off, right now?"

The euphemism made me smile.

Damian, a little nonplussed, said, "I'm in no hurry for you to leave, Mum."

And Kevin responded, "I'd go straight for your purse," and chuckled at his own joke.

When we went downstairs, so Mother could sleep, I said, "Do you think she was asking you both for permission to go?"

Damian looked a bit stricken, and said, "Oh God, do you think so?"

Kevin clenched his jaw and said nothing.

Ann called at 7:00 PM; she stayed away today. When the phone rang, Damian, downstairs, and I, upstairs, picked up the phone, simultaneously.

Ann said, "I'd like to speak to Mother, please."

Damian hung up, and I handed the phone over to Mother.

It seems Ann was just checking in, and I heard Mother say, "Of course, I missed seeing you dear."

When Mother dies, how will Ann fill the enormous gap? They have been part of each other's daily lives for so many years.

More tomorrow, it is 11:30, and I'm emotionally exhausted.

9:30 AM
26th June

And this morning Mother's awake, feeling cleansed. Much to my surprise, and delight, she greeted me with, "I'm so glad to have had a good cry. I didn't think I'd ever stop."

She even told Kevin about it, who responded, "I once read in the newspaper that in America *men* cry at least once, every four to six weeks. Can you imagine that? I can't even conceive of such a thing!"

Before I could contain it, a retort flew out of my mouth, "Presumably, you believe everything you read in the paper because you expect everyone to believe what *you* write."

He said nothing, and I thought later what an uncharitable and mean-spirited thing to say, but I didn't have the grace to apologize.

Mother wanted her hair washed this morning. She wasn't satisfied to have her scalp simply refreshed with a warm, damp sponge, which I do daily. It's been a few days since I shampooed her. So this was her first trip to the bathroom in her "chariot" for at least a week. As I cavorted with the commode chair to the bathroom, I introduced our tune, *In the Mood*, stopping for a salutary dip at the tall mirror on the landing. Ablutions are done and Mother is now sleeping. "I'll try not to ruin my hair-do," she says, as she nods off.

Four letters arrived today, all postmarked 23rd June, PM. All from you, and as yet unopened—until I can take an hour by myself, to revel in them; plus two cards from Anna, one with an exquisite poem, which touched me deeply. I am surrounded with such love, and two of you are actively expressing it. How grateful I am.

HB, do you know you are cherished? There are no words; though I keep trying to find them! It's quite indescribable, the infinite love I have for you. It fills me up, until it spills out through my pen, and spills out, and spills out.

Kisses,
Ju

♦   ♦   ♦

26th June
10:30 PM
In 'my' room

Hello Love,

St. Cuthbert's clock is striking the half hour.

I tucked Mother in at 10:00, and she's already sound asleep. Her breathing is audible from here.

The skylight is open, just a crack; the wind is whistling erratically in very ghostly sighs, and I am reveling in the cold night air blowing down on me as I write—though Damian and I felt quite chilled on our way back from the pub.

I just got off the phone with you, and am glad to hear you are going to see the doctor before the weekend. With Anna coming in, as early as 10:30 AM on Saturday, only thirty-six hours or so from now, you'll have had at least one chiropractic adjustment, and may have a couple of additional appointments booked.

Good to know you'll be at the café on the 4th. After dinner, everyone will want to go off to watch a firework display, and you can go home to bed and get some space and sleep. Please make sure Ollie is in the house as she's desperately afraid of fireworks.

This evening at 7:00, I readied Mother for bed as usual, which means propping her up in bed as high as I can manage, then preparing a warm, squeezed-out sponge with her favorite soap. I gently wash her face, neck, hands and arms. Then, while she brushes her teeth—spitting the residue into a little bowl—I go to the bathroom to scrub her partial plate, and then I brush her hair.

Tonight, as I soaped her face, she suddenly asked, "How old is your father?"

"Well, he'd be ninety-two now, if he'd lived," I replied—instantly realizing that she thought I was someone else.

"Oh!" she said, rather aghast, "I thought he was still alive!"

"No, he's not," says I then added, rather mischievously, "He was *your* husband, you know."

Her eyes flew wide open, like a startled doe. I chuckled, and kissed her on her soapy forehead, and said, laughingly, "I'm your daughter, Judith. Did you think you were talking to Chris? She was here this afternoon, working on your toenails. Remember?"

"Oh! *What* a faux pas, I've just made," she retorted, and we laughed and laughed, until we almost cried; when she paused for breath, she said, somewhat relieved, "Yes, I did think you were Chris. I wonder why I did that."

"Maybe because I'm washing your face and hands, and drying them, like Chris did your feet this afternoon. Perhaps you were just continuing the conversation with her, about her father?" (She'd told me earlier that they talked about Chris's father.)

"Oh, what a relief," she said, "I can't start mixing you up with the other caregivers."

I said I took it as a compliment, as I must seem as professional and competent as they are.

Her medications distort time, faces, places, names, and—thank goodness—ease her pain as well.

Damian says he can see the degradation of her condition in just two days. Kevin interjects, "She seems perfectly normal to me," Is he in denial again?

I'm tired tonight, as I imagine you are. I must sleep. (Wimbledon was rained out again today.)

10:00 AM

Mother is much more disoriented this morning, somewhat absent, and confused. As is usual now, she couldn't stand; it was very difficult getting her on and off the commode and back into her bed again—the most challenging, yet.

With her permission, I dressed her with one of the new, more absorbent, pads, as she is now incontinent and not aware of it. The smaller pads she's been wearing just aren't dense enough to absorb the uncontrolled volume.

I told Kevin she seemed more disoriented and, to illustrate the point, I mentioned a couple of things Mother said to me earlier, as in, "Did Kevin put the red coat back?" and "Was Judith warm enough last night?"

To which he responded, "She was dreaming, that's all."

Completely inappropriately, I said that it was probably more comforting for him to think that, whereupon he went upstairs to check on her himself, (though he didn't say that's what he was doing, that's just my mind, conjuring again). I could hear Mother's voice, rambling on, so muddled—about her sisters, and sundry other topics—and fully expected Kevin to come down with some grasp of my reality, but he didn't. He held firmly to his own, "She's perfectly normal," he said. Is it too painful for him to accept, or is he perhaps saying it for my benefit? So be it.

Mother couldn't remember how to brush her teeth this morning, and when she was on the commode I gave her toilet tissue to use. Instead of dropping it into the commode she handed it back to me with great care—like a precious gift. And Kevin says she's "perfectly normal." But then again, what is normal?

The need to constantly release my attachment to her, in every now, stares me in the face more and more forthrightly. I can see her exiting minute-by-minute.

I want to get this letter in the post by 10:30, so I'll end and give it to Kevin to take, as he's about to leave for the shops.

Today, for what I believe will be the last time, Mother will have her favorite meal—roast duck breast with orange sauce; sage and onion stuffing with gravy; petit pois peas, and new potatoes slathered with butter and parsley. She no longer feeds herself, as her right arm and hand has, according to her, "… forgotten what to do!"

I love you, sweetheart,
Ju

P.S. It's dry now, though wind and rain buffeted all night. The sun streams sporadically between the clouds, but not enough (as yet) to call it a sunny day.

◆   ◆   ◆

27th June
Friday
10:40 PM
In 'my' room

Hello dearest HB,

How luxurious to have such a long chat with you on the phone today.

An amazing event unfolded when I returned from speaking with you. It was time for Mother's lemon tea and 3:00 PM medication, so when it was made, I took it up. She was sleeping, and awoke as the floor creaked underfoot.

It seems the locum phoned while I was out. Damian was in the room with Mother at the time. The locum said she'd stopped by on Tuesday at lunch time, but couldn't get any reply to her knocking on the door. She assumed no-one was in and went away. The mind boggles. According to Damian, Mother told the locum that she'd had pain this morning, and that I'd given her an extra pill, and was authorized to do it—quite so. Mother couldn't remember the pill by name. The locum also asked if Mother would like her to visit today, and Mother replied, "No thank you. Judith is taking care of me." Her own loved doctor is due back from the Scilly Isles tomorrow.

As Mother sipped the steaming tea, I could see she was pondering. Eventually, she said very thoughtfully, "I think I'll go tonight!" And she looked into my eyes with such a tender expression.

When she said this, I was sitting on the commode chair next to her bed.

She continued, "I know you don't want me to go, but I really want to."

I reached across and took her hand, and looking directly into her calm, blue eyes, I said, with absolute truth, "Mother, I know I can be selfish, but I'm not selfish enough to want anything other than what is best for you, and if you choose tonight, God speed, and a blissful journey."

"Thank you, dear," she said, squeezing my hand, then with a twinkle in her eye, she added, "Unless I wake up in the morning," and she chuckled.

She sipped more tea saying, "Delicious, delicious," and took her pills; then looking heavenwards she whispered in an entreating tone, "Please! Please! Please!"

We finished our tea, and I left her to sleep.

At about 5:00 PM, TA arrived. She very kindly brought Ann, Mother, and me, a miniature rose bush. No doubt, Ann will enjoy all three when Mother has gone and I've returned home. Meanwhile, two are in Mother's room. TA also brought Kevin a bottle of whiskey, which he swiftly, and discreetly, secreted away in his little grip bag. TA climbed the stairs and I soon heard the sound of kisses in mutual greeting, and then TA's voice crying, "Oh, your arms are *so thin* Enid!"

It must have shocked TA to see Mother's debilitation. Damian went up to join them and, soon after, Ann.

Later, when I collected Mother's supper tray, I said that everyone was welcome to stay, as long as Mother didn't mind them seeing her on the commode. Mother instantly said, "I'd like my privacy, please."

I'd told Ann what Mother said earlier, about possibly going tonight, and asked her if she'd like some time alone with her; she did. Mother mused later, "Ann seemed down, tonight."

After Ann left, TA and Damian visited with Mother, again, until eventually, they left for supper and to check into the B & B. Mother slept for a while.

I was sitting quietly downstairs, in perfect stillness and peace, when, shockingly, coming directly from the stairwell, I heard my *father's* voice calling me with the greatest sense of urgency, "JUDITH!" His call was so loud! I leapt to my feet, ran into the hall with my heart pounding, stopping to listen again. It was so clearly my *father's* voice; a shudder rolled down my spine as I flew up the stairs, two and three at a time, and found Mother gasping for air, squeaking, "I can't breathe, I can't breathe."

With adrenalin surging, I hauled her up and stuffed pillows behind her, to keep her as erect as possible and, within seconds, her breathing became less labored. A few minutes later she had recovered, and in a very small voice, said, "I was quite frightened; I couldn't call, and I couldn't sit myself up."

I chose to say nothing about my father's voice alerting me to her need. Amazing! He died twenty-one years ago, but there is no doubt that his energy came in on a frequency I was tuned to. Mother sat up for the rest of the evening, more erect than usual, and listened to the first and second part of another Rosamund Pilcher story; part three and four are ready for tomorrow, if she's still here.

At 10:00, I placed her on the commode. She had a small bowel movement, the first since Sunday.

When I tucked her up for the night, hugging and kissing her as usual, I told her I loved her and wished her a blissful journey—should she choose to go tonight. She thanked me and added, "God bless you, Judith. I love you all around the world and down the plug hole." (This was something her father used to say to her when she was a child, meaning—infinitely).

I asked whether she'd like me to sleep on the chair in her room (which converts to a single bed), but she said, no, she didn't want me to do that, and added, "I'll call you if need be."

She knows I'll be there instantly.

Right now, I'm sitting up in bed, wondering whether I'll be called; the three to four nightly checks I do may be enough. I hope so.

Change of subject: I called work to ask for leave-of-absence forms to be sent to me here. The woman at the Call Center realized I was calling from England, and said, "Oh, my parents are in Whitby, right now!" She seemed pleased to share the connection, as though, in telling me, her parents felt closer. I didn't think to ask her to send the forms via airmail; sure hope she does. I'm requesting a new leave, as the allowed twelve-week leave that I'm on will expire on 14th July. I used four of the twelve last year, (when Mother was hospitalized) and the other eight are quickly whittling away. I'm planning to request up to twelve weeks more; this should cover every eventuality. Should Mother go in the next hour or the next week, I'll still need a couple of weeks here. I don't think I'll need to stay longer than that after the funeral. Two weeks should be time enough, to remove all Mother's personal belongings, and prepare the house for sale. She has instructed us to show the house furnished.

Ann plans to take home two or three small pieces of furniture that Mother has already given to her. Kevin says if Ann doesn't want the rest, and the buyers don't want the house furnished, he wants it. I suggested he might rent a van to transport it to Spain, and he said, "Oh, I hadn't thought of that!" Perhaps he hadn't thought that far ahead. My problem-solving skills are rearing up, and my mind is taking me out into the future, so frequently. So be it. Be present, Judith! Be present!

I sure hope you saw the chiropractor again today. Soon you'll be with Anna, Jordan and Jack—*sans moi*—and, by the time you read this, everyone will have already left you, and returned to their own homes!

It's 11:15 PM, and I need to catch some shut eye. More tomorrow!

28th June
Saturday

This morning, Mother is alive and cheerful. She ate a good breakfast and is now on an increased dose of the painkiller, as pain filled her body again this morning.

At 10:00, Damian and TA are off to visit TA's niece, and Damian says he'll be back here, without TA, tomorrow night.

Yesterday, I was serving coffee, tea, wine, or meals, on and off all day, for Kevin, Father Jim, Damian and TA, Mother, and myself—perhaps almost as busy as you have been, with all my children there. You and I are very much in service to those we love right now.

HB, since my arrival and subsequent care of Mother, I want to share with you the clarity I've gained about the essential nature of giving compassionate care: despite my chattering mind's resistance to death; disease; odorous feces; bloody urine, and the general helplessness that sickness and aging can bring, it is abundantly clear to me, now, that to give truly compassionate care it is essential to acknowledge the ego—permeated as mine is with its petty judgments—and consciously set it aside. By doing that and, at the same time, quieting my mind, an eternal inner stillness is revealed, from which conscious, compassionate care flows. Mother says she has "never—even as an infant," felt as nurtured as she does now; and the source of that nurture is the eternal stillness within.

Must catch the post, I love you,
Ju

◆   ◆   ◆

28th June
11:30 AM
In the sitting room

Dearest HB,

Despite the increased dose of pain medication, Mother is still in pain. If it hasn't diminished within half an hour, I have permission to give her another 10 mg.

Hazel came in. She said, quite confidently, that Mother is waiting for her own doctor to return from his holiday, and that Mother will be "gone by next weekend." I told Hazel about my father's voice, alerting me to Mother's breathing crisis yesterday, to which she immediately responded, "He saved her because he knows she's waiting for her doctor to come back!"

I love Hazel. She's so caring, coupled with a pragmatism that I find admirable—though someone else might not consider acknowledgement of my dead father's voice pragmatic. She has no doubt at all that the energy of the departed moves about and visits the living. She related several stories to me, about ghosts and spirits, though refrained from using either of those words. At Mother's request, I gave Hazel our two miniature rose bushes—a gift of gratitude.

Ann came for lunch, but unfortunately, she took Kevin's silence personally and decided not to stay. Kevin is in his own world, coping the best way he knows how, and I imagine not giving either of his sisters a single thought. We are all doing our best.

Did I tell you that TA also brought Mother some caviar? Mother's preference is for soft roes, but she said, "I'll try the caviar. I don't want to hurt TA's feelings."

So, as an *hors d'oeuvres*, I gave her half a teaspoon of caviar on one soldier of toast. She *loved* it, and immediately asked for more and finished it all, as her main meal.

Have I told you lately that your presence is missed? Though, in truth, my heart is fully engaged all day, from 6:40 AM to 10:00 PM, and I'm not aware of taking a conscious moment to *dwell* on missing you. It is now, when I write to you, that the awareness of our physical separation leaches up. Our daily phone call and your letters are so treasured.

Damian and TA left, and I finally got their plans straight. Damian will be back tomorrow, TA will be back for Monday and Tuesday nights, when they both leave for Greece, on Wednesday. They intend to return here on the 11th, and fly home to France, via Geneva, on the 15th—no matter what.

Music on the Green is in full flood; all day yesterday, and all of today. The music is so loud we can hear it through the open skylights. Last night, at eleven o'clock, I listened to the fireworks whooshing skyward and bursting light into the night. Mother didn't hear any of it; I checked her on several occasions, and each time she slept peacefully.

It seems Wimbledon may be cancelled completely, or have to go to a third week—the decision is to be made later. Back soon!

9:10 PM

I called you a while ago to hear that Anna, Jordan, and Jack have arrived there safely. You sounded stressed. Already! I trust you will take care of yourself and take the space you need.

While writing, I'm half-watching a repeat of a 1988 episode of *Inspector Morse*. John Thaw looks very young, and Kevin Whately, as Sergeant Lewis, looks about twenty years old.

Mother's body finally produced a monumentally successful bowel movement; however, she has forgotten how to clean herself, so I'm doing that for her. She doesn't seem to mind at all, surrendering, as always, without a murmur of grumbling or complaint.

I set up parts three and four of the book that Mother started last night—Rosamund Pilcher's, *Another View*, and heard intermittent comments coming from her bedroom, "Marvelous! Marvelous!"

This evening, she is listening to a Perry Como tape. She is great fan of Perry. She and I went to see him in concert, twenty-plus years ago, when she and Ann came to stay, following my father's death.

Wimbers is on! I watched four superb matches, fifth-set-cliff-hangers, all welcome, though brief distractions between administering dear Mother's medication, commode use and pad changes.

29th June
Sunday
9:40 AM

Mother is in pain again. I gave her the increased dosage, but by 9:15 it still hadn't alleviated the pain, so remembering that her doctor was due home this weekend, I called him on his home number. He answered the phone, and said he'd just walked in from his holidays. I asked, "Are you on duty?"

"No, not until tomorrow—and I don't know who is."

I asked him if he'd prefer me to call the emergency number, and he replied, "Yes. Unless there's something I can do for you on the phone."

I told him the situation, and he authorized me to give an additional 10 mg of the pain medication in the morning and evening, and that he'll be in to see Mother this week. I emphasized, "Sooner, rather than later would be really good," and I added that Mother seems somewhat confused. To this he responded that it is not due to the medication but the debilitation of her mind, caused by the cancer. (This surprised me.) After a short pause, he continued, "Perhaps it's time for your mother to have immediate-release morphine," and said that he'd write a prescription, and we hung up.

So now Mother's taken another 10 mg, and she's listening to meditation music. She is completely incontinent now. There is much cleaning up of her body to do, before, after, and in-between commode use. She has the added scourge of constant diarrhea, which is surely better than the bowel blockage, which is how all this started almost a year ago. Dear, dear, Mother!

This morning as I conducted her ablutions—she can no longer do any of them for herself, not even clean her teeth—she enquired of me, "Where do you come from, originally?"

"Erdington," I replied, in a matter-of-fact tone.

"You *do*! Well, that's where *we* are all from, I'm *amazed*!"

And so it is.

Later, I was in the bathroom applying my mascara, when Kevin went in to see her. I overheard Mother telling him, "Judith comes from Erdington, isn't that amazing!" Then she added, "She's a good girl, I don't know what I would do without her." (A girl?)

Kevin's reply came swiftly, "But then you would be relying on me, instead!"

I almost stuck the mascara wand in my eye. Kevin has not commented on Mother's condition since.

Hazel's arrived, and it's time to make coffee. I'll finish this letter now. Mother asked me to give you her love, and also please pass her love on to Anna, Jordan, and Jack. This may be the last message to them from her and, by the time you get this, they may all have left the Sanctuary already, and certainly will have, if the post takes the usual ten days to get there. And Mother may have left by then, also.

I notice that when Mother is in pain, I feel nauseous. (A somewhat similar experience to the time my English setter, China, gave birth to her first litter of pups—thirty years ago—and I felt contractions throughout the pups' delivery. The vet said it was psychosomatic.) I imagine the nausea will subside when Mother dies, and perhaps before, if the pain in her eyes retreats. That's what my body is responding to, the expression in her eyes. Her focus is turned inward. Perhaps she is managing the pain that way.

When Ann called just now, Mother told her, "The pain was dreadful earlier, but it's easing now." I find it challenging to disassociate from Mother's pain. I keep focusing on surrendering to what is, and keep breathing, consciously. I have the deepest empathy for her.

Later,

Ju

Same day
10:15 PM
Sitting in bed

Hello Love,

I'm tired tonight. This was a very bad day for Mother, yet she put on an amazingly good front for all her visitors. They seemed to come in droves—Kevin, Hazel, Ann, Vincent, (with Communion), and then, again, Ann, Kevin, then TA and Damian, and Damian again, alone. Then Norah, Mother's sister, called at 4:00 PM.

In between all these visits, dear Mother had the usual commode breaks, medications, coffee, lunch, tea, supper, and glasses of wine. She also listened to a book on tape and, while I was on the phone with you, she had another breathless emergency; this one addressed by Kevin. She was very short of breath all day.

Her pain hasn't quite subsided, so if she still has a vestige of it in the morning, I'll ask her doctor to write the prescription for instant-release morphine. Surprisingly, her food intake is unimpaired.

I find the smoke from Damian's cigarettes congesting. The skylight at the top of the stairs is kept open now, drawing the spiraling smoke out and away from Mother's room, and I open the patio door to keep the air flowing, to freshen up the house. Each time I leave to tend to Mother, the patio door gets closed—by whomever. It is quite chilly and smoky inside. But I won't ask Damian to smoke outside. It's Mother's house, and she would *never* ask him to do that.

The headache I had when we spoke hasn't worsened. Thank goodness it hasn't developed into a full-blown migraine.

I read in the local newspaper that on Tuesday, 1st July, for six hours, starting at 8:00 AM, the water will be turned off for some repairs, up the road. That means I'll have to complete my own and Mother's ablutions by 7:00 AM, then fill up the kettle, kitchen sink, and bathtub, so we will have the ability to flush the toilet. It will be an added challenge, to wash out and disinfect the commode without any running water; this is usually done at least six times by 2:00 PM. Such is the latest challenge set by the local Council. Hazel says she will manage fine with a kettle of hot water. All this assumes that Mother will still be with us on Tuesday.

Damian ate supper with us, and TA went off to see an aunt, half an hour's drive from here.

Early tomorrow morning, TA is leaving the B & B to drive to Shropshire, to see other relatives. Damian is staying on at the B & B until 7:00 AM on Wednesday morning, when he plans to take the bus to the airport, to catch the 2:30 flight to Greece. Must be nice! (Oh! Here's my chattering little mind again.)

At this point, I'm thinking the funeral need not be delayed to suit Damian's travel schedule. He'll either make it back or he won't. Maybe Kevin, and I, along with Norah, and her daughter, Sarah, will be the only ones there. (Oh! Listen to the mental noise. It is quite hilarious when observed in action.)

Ann is "completely and utterly exhausted." Notwithstanding that, she and I managed to thoroughly enjoy the Henman vs. Haarhus tennis match.

I've been here almost five weeks. The doctor was right to suggest my coming here when he did; the daily decline in Mother's condition is so evident.

This morning, Kevin said to me, "I do hope no one is going to be maudlin, and make a lot of noise when Mother goes!" I looked at him, felt my lips compress and my nostrils flare and, with a great effort, said absolutely nothing—out loud; my mind did overtime on that comment.

Today, when Ann came in to visit Mother, she told her about the Hong Kong political fracas that's been in the news the last two days—telling me, as she came downstairs, "Mother needs to know what's going on in the world."

Later, after a chat with Mother, Damian came downstairs and said in an incredulous tone, "Mother doesn't remember what the village looks like! Amazing, isn't it?"

He seems more at peace than Kevin, with the imminence of Mother's death, but hasn't quite fathomed her mind's confusion. She makes such a gigantic effort to engage in intelligent conversation when anyone visits her, except me. Our relationship continues to be effortless for us both, and I am filled with gratitude for our intimacy, and the trust with which she surrenders to whatever state is present for her.

Her breathing is very shallow today. She told me how she would like to take a deep, satisfying breath, or heave a great sigh. But she can't and most likely won't again. She's always feared suffocating, and I'm hoping that whatever the doctor gives her will help her breathing become less labored. But that may not be possible.

Change of subject: I cannot even imagine going back to work right away when I return. The culture shock will be more than I want to manage, with any semblance of normalcy, and I want a little time to transition back into my life with you. I shall talk to Nicole about it, after Mother's gone.

The laundry, washed yesterday, is still not dry—it's hanging on the rack in this bedroom. Do I appreciate all the labor and time saving devices we have? Yes! Nothing can be taken for granted. Conscious gratitude is ever present within me.

It's 11:15 PM, and I must check on Mother then get some sleep—more, later.

I love you—lots of kisses
Ju

30th June
8:00 AM

A year ago, today, Mother and I flew back from her last vacation at our Sanctuary.

Before dawn I heard her groaning, and tiptoed in. She was having great difficulty breathing and was completely parched. I bolstered her up and gave her small sips of water, and she went back to sleep until 5:30, when we repeated the procedure. As usual, she couldn't put even a modicum of weight on her feet. I somehow managed to get her on to the commode and back into bed. She's so breathless. She wants the doctor to come in today, but says she doesn't want me to call him!

Kevin is with her now, while I finish my ablutions. I have a feeling that today will be very, very long. (So of course it will be; what we focus on expands!)

A letter came, mailed the day you got back from the Cape, postmarked the 25th June. Thank you, sweetheart.

I love you,
Ju

◆   ◆   ◆

30th June
9:50 AM
In the sitting room

Hello HB,

Mother's right arm is very weak; nevertheless, she is still in good spirits. I called her doctor. He's coming.

Damian, he's with Mother now, declared that if the funeral takes place when he's on holiday in Greece he will not come to back for it, but if it's on the 11th, 12th, 13th, or 14th July, he will.

Kevin is also thinking about whether he'll stay for it, as his ticket is for the 4th. Should Mother die by the 3rd, he may just use his original flight reservation. He's considering. Ann has made it clear she will not be attending. Mother completely understood when Ann told her she just couldn't face the ordeal. So our Aunt Norah, her daughter, Sarah, and I, may be the only family attending.

At first, my siblings' decisions floored me. Even though I now accept their choices, my first reactive thought was that they are just thinking about their own convenience, and not at all what Mother would want. But whatever they want to do, I know Mother would completely support them. Perhaps, by not attending, they avoid having their pain on display, another assumption of course. What do I know? My thoughts about it aren't important. My siblings are taking care of themselves in the way that they need, as am I. So be it.

I've come to a decision that I found challenging to make. Despite Mother's request that I do so, I've decided not to have a post funeral reception for her local friends and neighbors. This is only the second request that she's made that I'm consciously choosing not to fulfill. I'm not willing to deal with all the food prep-aration, and greeting guests, and listening to genuine, hand-wringing expressions of sympathy. I feel too vulnerable. (Ah! Not wanting my own grief to be pub-lic—how I project my own vulnerability onto my siblings!) And especially, (she says, rationalizing everything) if my brothers have gone home, and I'm here on my own, having to clean up after everyone, and throw away uneaten food ... when all I'll want to do is curl up in a fetal position, and surf the salty tides of grief. This is selfish I know, but it is what I'm choosing. I told Mother, with my apologies. She was completely accepting.

Ann came round at 5:30, and stayed upstairs until Mother succumbed to the higher dose of medication. When Ann came down to the kitchen she was some-what distraught, and whispered, "Mother's breathing is much slower. She's dying!"

Kevin and Damian were watching tennis.

Perhaps this is the first time that Ann has been with Mother when the latter has gone into a deep, pain-free sleep, and appears to be comatose. I went upstairs, with Ann tiptoeing behind me, her expression stricken; we stood together qui-etly, observing Mother's breathing: inhale ... long exhale ... long pause ... inhale ... long exhale ... longer pause ... inhale ... long exhale ... an even longer pause

… inhale … and so on. Ann mouthed across the room to me, "This is *hideous*, no one should have to go through this."

I empathize with Ann's pain. And in this moment, this is what is—and taking action is all there is left—either withdraw from the situation, accept it without judgment, or change one's perception of it.

After waking Mother and giving her the seven o'clock medication, I left Ann alone with her. Twenty minutes later, Ann came down, weeping quietly, "Mother said good-bye to me. I think she will die tonight!"

Totally reactively, I blurted out, "She's said good-bye the last three nights in a row!" Not the best comforting technique! I wanted to retract the words instantly, but they were out. Immediately, Ann gathered her things and left. I followed her to the gate, to latch it behind her as usual, and offered, "If Mother dies tonight do you want me to come round, or call you?"

"I don't want *you* to do *anything!*" she cried, and dashed off. She was so upset, her grief palpable; exacerbated by one untamed, voiced thought.

I went up to Mother, and there she lay; eyes *shining*. She was *jubilant!* She cried out to me, "Judith, I reconciled with Ann! Everything is cleared up between us, *after a whole lifetime!*"

HB, she was *pure radiance!*

Filled with wonder at her joy, I asked if she wanted to talk about it, or if she preferred to keep it private, and she said, "If I talk about it, I may cry."

"You choose," I offered.

Then she began, "We both cried! I just said, Ann, come and give me a kiss, because I'm going to die tonight, and *she did!* Can you imagine? Then we said a lot of things to each other and *everything* is alright now."

I kissed her warm brow, and held her hand, saying, "Oh Mother, I'm so very happy for you both," then asked, "Did you say good-bye to her?"

"No," came her reply, "Not good-bye. I really expect to see her again." Then, looking right into my eyes, she asked, "I *am* getting everything cleared up, aren't I?"

I felt such joy for her, "It certainly looks that way. Will you be able to die in peace, now?"

"Yes, I think I'm getting there." Her eyes twinkled, and she beamed with an amazing luminosity. She was completely lucid throughout the entire conversation.

I washed her face and hands, cleaned her teeth and partial plate, and brushed her hair. She refused the commode, saying, "Later."

I think she is becoming accustomed to the security of the pads.

Now, she's listening to the third and fourth parts of *Snow in April*, by Rosamund Pilcher.

For the first time she's taken 90 mg of painkiller, and she may zone out through the whole book.

I'm so very happy for her that she has reconciled with Ann. She's truly *elated*. Such a blessing!

More later,

Same day
10:20 PM

When I went in just now, for Mother to use the commode for the last time tonight, she was still elated—even after listening to a book on tape for one and a half hours. She said, with her eyes still shining with joy, "We really achieved something today!"

"Does it feel like you and Ann have run a marathon together?"

"Yes! Like finishing a marathon together," she beamed again in response, her face glowing, and years seem to have shed from her.

She asked me, as though she is leaving on the *best* trip of a life-death time, "Do you think I'll go tonight, Judith?"

"Can you think of any reason to stay?" I asked.

"Do you think I've done *everything* now?"

"Do you?"

"Yes! I think I must have. It was all so spontaneous, and *right*."

As she lay on her pillows and relaxed, I kissed her.

Then it was time for her to say something to me, "Judith, *we* did this today. Your support was here all the time. I couldn't have done it without you. Thank you for *everything*, for today and for every day, and for all the things you do that I don't see. I'm so grateful for *all* you've done, *with* me, and *for* me."

I kissed her soft cheek again, and she kissed mine, beaming into my eyes, the sweetest, most embracing, all-encompassing gaze. What an amazing woman! Such a generous spirit!

"You're welcome, Mother, and I'd do it all again."

"Thank you, dear. God bless. Good-bye darling."

"Good-bye, Mother. God bless."

I went to my room and gently closed the door, my heart overflowing. The tears came, with joy, with grief, for all of this precious intimacy with her. My whole being overflows with love for her. And now she's gently snoring, under the influence of 90 mg of painkiller and two sleeping pills. She may release her spirit tonight—and she may not.

I love you, HB—how can I ever thank you for your love and support for my being here?

More tomorrow,

◆   ◆   ◆

The gifts presented during June came so thick and fast, I sometimes felt over-whelmed. It was impossible to absorb them all, let alone integrate them. Writing home so frequently, however, allowed me to chronicle, with a deep sense of won-der, not only each precious moment with my mother, but also the emptying of my noisy mind; my roller-coasting emotions, and my ego's surging needs—even as they arose.

Sharing these details as they unfolded, provided an opening through which conscious awareness kept flowing. Without this conscious awareness, the peace and stillness essential to serve my mother would have been absent.

Enid aged 17, with her brother, Keith, and the twins

Nena Mina (right) and Lola, in Santander

Enid aged 19

Phil aged 27

Enid and Phil, soon after their marriage, in the garden of their home

Mother, with Ann, Kevin and Damian   Mother, holding Judith

From left to right: Damian, Judith, Ann, and Kevin, in Ryton,
with Mother aged 30, and my father, in the uniform of the Home Guard

Mother aged 42

Mother aged 04, taken shortly before she took to her bedroom, for the duration

Mother and Kevin, photo taken on 18th June, at Norah's request

4

Into the Silence

1st July
Tuesday
8:10 AM

Hi dear HB,

Mother is still here. I got up at 5:40 AM, to complete all major water usage before 8:00. The Water Board has turned off the water—until 2:00 PM, so they say.

It's fortunate that I rose early, as another rather extravagant case of diarrhea occurred in the night, and Mother knew nothing about it, until I swished back the bed clothes. It took a good half hour to clean, wash, change, gently hoist, push, pull, roll, until she was spotlessly clean. Then I bundled all the soiled linen and clothing into the bathroom, rinsed it all out, and loaded the washing machine, hoping to complete the wash cycle before we lost water. Mother was most apologetic, and we conjectured that the organic fig-and-malt bread that she ate yesterday, might have contributed, and her catharsis with Ann may also have released years of retention.

Mother is still elated about her conversation with Ann, "I can't eat much breakfast this morning," she says, and keeps exclaiming, "What a monumental day!"

She's also completely pain free and, as I write, is snoozing sublimely.

Now, whenever anyone leaves her room, she says, "Good-bye."

Her year of preparation seems to be winding to a close—may her minutes, hours, and days tick by in stillness and peace.

What a wonderful blessing it is, to be a part of this—Mother's dying process, experienced *fully* by her. It all serves to deepen my awareness of our purpose here, to dive into life in the present moment, with an open heart, and just *be*.

We are enjoying the first prolonged sun since the 10th June. When I emerged from sleep at 4:30 I felt a lightness of spirit dwelling within, and opened my eyes to a cloudless, vast, blue sky beyond the skylight.

The migraine has almost gone. It will have left completely by noon, seventy-two hours to the minute. I can't fathom how I ingested any dairy products—and wonder if I'll ever let this allergy go.

A letter came from you this morning; thank you for writing each and every day. Your letters are utterly important to my well-being—to touch something you've recently touched; read your words; thoughts; feelings; actions; all written with your own pen, held in your strong, suntanned, hand. You mailed the letter that came this morning on 25th June, and it took only seven days to arrive, including the weekend. None of your news is old news. A letter from you comes in a new present moment. Bless you, love.

Hong Kong was handed over yesterday by the Brits, to the Chinese. There was much televised coverage. That, and Wimbers, served as distractions between ministrations to Mother, Kevin and Damian. The language of the Hong Kong reporters was revealing. "Hong Kong people are being handed over to their new *masters* or new *rulers*." Questions posed to the public in on-the-spot-interviews, included, "Aren't you *afraid* of the Chinese police and military, who are *pouring into the city* from Beijing as we speak?" Interviews, with the "ousted" legislative body, who are "pro-democracy," elicited the prompted negative emotions. Though I'm fully aware that it is a choice how the interviewees respond, they were certainly led down the path laid out by the reporter's choice of words.

The propaganda, about the British rule for 150 years, "putting commerce and wealth into the hands of the Hong Kong people," was over the top. Just last week, the BBC was televising from HK, doing pre-handover coverage. They showed eight men, sleeping and living each day in a false-ceilinged, mezzanine-type area, which was added to the building in which they lived in order to cram more renters into an already overcrowded space. Double layers of men, squatting on their haunches, no head room, eating rice from a bowl—"wealth" into the hands of the HK people? Some hands may be. The self-deception evident in the language used, and the images presented, was as plain as an ass on a goat. I listened to the words and phrases, and my interpretation is—for the Brits read good guys, with their benevolent patriarchy, and for the Chinese read, expect suppression by the bad guys. I find it quite astonishing to listen to the (perhaps unconscious) subliminal messages being broadcast. Now, how's that for righteous indignation! So be it.

This is a long letter, so many pages. I hope you're sitting comfortably with a cup of tea, or a glass of wine. You've an opportunity to relax for quite a while, wading through this letter.

HB, I find it challenging being away from you for so long. All in divine right order, however. So be it.

Rereading this letter, it sure roams between the profound and the trivial. So much happens—we happen so much—in the course of life and death. How rich and full this earth-school is, a never-ending source of complete wonder. Over the span of a few days, I go from the weeds, to diarrhea; to writing a letter and reading yours; hearing my dead father's voice; making a bed, having the most intimate of conversations—all in the moment—then the mind skips away mulling about the future, as though it existed. Everything that comes to my attention fills me with joy and wonder. How blessed we are to be sharing this adventure of life, together.

Kisses, I adore you, and love you,
Ju

♦   ♦   ♦

1st July
10:00 PM
In bed

Hello Love,

I sat with Mother from 9:00 to 9:30, tonight. She listened to a book on tape, *A Year in Provence*, read by the author, Peter Mayle. She was not aware that I was in the room, and for the last ten minutes of the second part she laughed and chuckled; her eyes closed. At the same time, she appeared to be deeply asleep which, if she was, seemed to provide further evidence that the consciousness of a sleeping body can hear voices, and experience, on an emotional level, what is being heard.

When I lifted her on to the commode afterwards, she said, "You know, I am so enjoying myself! It sounds funny, doesn't it? But, I really *am*!"

She is a miracle.

TA came in at 8:00 PM, and spent fifteen minutes with Mother, showing her photos of a vacation she and Damian enjoyed in Tunisia, a few weeks ago. Mother cannot see very well, but peers at them, and makes approving comments.

Damian was pleased with himself at suppertime. He fed Mother her dessert and was so chuffed to have "done something to help." Bless his heart. It hasn't occurred to me to ask either of my brothers if they want to do more to help. So be it, they'll offer, if they do.

Paul came in, it is his 43rd birthday, and he'd received cards from Mother and Ann, which delighted him. He drank a glass of Rioja with Kevin then took one up to Mother, and another for himself. He and Mother were laughing together. Despite her debilitated condition, she puts forth a great effort to be social with everyone, other than Hazel, Rachel and me.

Hazel came back to the house tonight, off-duty, with a bunch of sweet peas out of her garden. Their seductive bouquet permeates Mother's room. Hazel's so very kind and told me this morning, that Mother is "a replacement for the grandmother" she "never knew."

Between ministrations, I watched Wimbers. Becker is through to another round. Henman's match was stopped, due to lack of light—he's ahead 2 sets to 1 in the fourth round against Krjcek; the winner of the men's singles at Wimbers, last year.

It was so good to speak with you twice today. Tonight, I'm really tired and feeling bereft without you—and projecting into the future, I'm aware that my grieving will deepen into a bottomless chasm when Mother goes. It's what is. Surrender again, Judith.

I need to sleep; more tomorrow.

Kisses and hugs, I love you sweetheart,

10:20 AM
2nd July
Wednesday

Sándor is due to arrive there today! Kevin is out shopping. Wendy is with Mother, bathing her.

I woke with another migraine, more intense than the last one. I'll be glad when I can be away from cheese, yogurt, and breads made with dairy products. A residue of lactose, or casein, must be in invisible places; I don't know how to avoid it. I'm even more obsessive now, about washing all kitchen cloths daily, swabbing down the kitchen counters, and drinking from a single, commandeered mug.

Mother told me this morning that each night, for several nights now, she's been having the same dream. She described her dream as, "… too beautiful to tell, and too private to tell; and it's filling in all the gaps. *It is so beautiful.*" She whispered the latter with such reverence, and began to weep.

I sat quietly on her bed, and she reached for my hand, kissing it before holding it to her soft, warm cheek. In deep silence, for several minutes, we sat thus, her tears flowing. Then, she placed my hand on her coverlet, reached for a tissue and patted her eyes dry, smiling at me, with such love. She said nothing more about it.

I washed her hair in bed this morning, a warm, moistened sponge, smoothed all over her scalp. Then, using foaming gel and a little hairspray, I styled it—as usual. Her hair has grown in length, and is so baby-fine it flies about her head, wispy-wispy, ash-blonde, like a young girl's halo. She finds it nurturing to have Olay smoothed on her face and neck each morning, and a dab of Chanel #5 on her pulse points—now all part of our routine.

I just left you for a moment, to give Mother a requested commode-break, and she announced that she doesn't want Wendy, or Rachel, or Hazel, to help her with the commode use again—just me. So, as soon as Wendy left, she needed to urinate. She mentioned her dream again, "It was so *beautiful* I thought I was going to die this morning."

Wendy commented on Mother's lungs, which are now emitting a soft rattling sound. As I saw her out to her car, Wendy told me, "That sound is a sure sign of progression."

She also said that the subcutaneous syringe-driver, for the instant-release morphine, will take Mother into a deeper and deeper sleep, until she just "slips away." Mother would like to avoid the syringe-driver if possible, saying she doesn't want a needle in her again—unless the pain gets too bad. And as long as she can swallow her pills she won't need to have it.

At about 9:00 this morning, Damian and TA came in to say, "Good-bye." Before they went upstairs I suggested that they avoid saying "See you on the 11th," to Mother (when they are due to return for three days), so Mother won't feel any subconscious obligation, or need, to wait.

Here's another recent awareness: I'm witnessing how respectfully I'm keeping Mother's home, the way she has always kept it. A weekly polish for the furniture; carpets vacuumed at least twice a week; the bathtub, basin, and toilet are scrubbed several times daily; the cushions on the armchairs and sofa are plumped up each and every time someone leaves the room; the instant he leaves the house, Damian's ever-filled ashtray is emptied, then washed, dried, and put away; no dirty dishes are left in the kitchen sink—or left to drain—and the counter top and sink are always shined dry. My awareness included that the respect I'm referring to, may have been what Lucie felt, when she'd say to you, "Your father would or wouldn't like ... this or that." Perhaps how she kept things, or did things, was out of respect for him, rather than a lack of self-determination, as I recall thinking previously. It was thinking about Lucie that prompted me to share this with you. Keeping things the way Mother likes them, serves her, even though she doesn't see it.

Except for my time with you when I'm writing a letter, or we're on the phone, I'm administering to Mother most of the time, yet somehow I manage to watch Wimbers, or horse racing. They are pure distractions, in the present moment, which I thoroughly enjoy, and they do rein in my mind, from flying off into the future.

I'm off now, to get this in the post. Thank you so much, my love, for your letter posted 27th June.

Many thousands of kisses, I love you,
Ju

◆   ◆   ◆

2nd July
10:00 PM
Already in bed

Hi Sweetheart,

I've been here five weeks today!

Pour yourself a glass of wine and relax while you read this. I need to be in touch with someone who is familiar with my world, and you are it—forever.

Mother listened to the third part of *A Year in Provence,* and at 8:00 PM, she called me in to say, with great urgency, "It is being read too fast, I need to go to sleep for the night, *now*." She used the commode, (her third bowel movement today), then swallowed 90 mg of painkiller, and her sleeping pills. She was out like an ebbed tide by 8:30. Then Ann called.

The next paragraphs are a grumbling session, my ego needs to surface, so I'll let it exercise itself for a while, knowing you will skip this part if you don't want to hear me going on and on. I feel the need to let it out, somewhere where it will do no harm, or I shall lie awake and stew about it.

I'd invited Ann out for supper at 6:00, but she declined. At 8:30, by which time I'd eaten, she came round and wanted to go to the Globe for a talk, so we went. She had a lot on her mind. Her naked pain poured forth—at Mother's condition, having to see her declining every day, at losing her, "She ought to die now. Doesn't she know we've all done our best? How can she do this to us? I'm not sleeping. I need to sleep. I can't even have a day in bed, because someone always trips the fire alarm, and none of the others in the house know how to turn it off."

(Mea culpa—when I burned the toast this morning, it accidentally tripped the ultra-sensitive fire alarm, in the main house.)

Ann continued, "Once Mother's gone, her executor will be hounding me every day for a year wanting this and that. Damian's cigarette smoke made me feel sick in the middle of the night—for two nights in a row. I'm seriously thinking of taking up smoking again! *You* don't need to be here, there are Hospice services that do everything. Why don't you go back to your *beloved husband* and get on with your life. Mother should go into a hospital, *now*."

By 9:45, I felt such resistance to all that was being said that, seeking to stem the rising tide within, I distracted my heart from her pain-filled words by witnessing my mind take its own dark turn, and it thought that Ann would have made a *fortune* as a comedienne. Her thinking continued taking hairpin bends, spawned, no doubt, by the bottomless pit of pain she is experiencing for all that Mother is suffering, yet, in the moment, when Ann was saying all this, I was able to step away somehow, and realized that if I was in the audience at a comedy show, her words, put into a stage performance context, could be perceived as absolutely hilarious—depending on one's brand of humor. Such is the way of minds—but not of hearts. I feel her pained heart, but cannot take it on. My own is enough.

Here's some more judgmental grumbling: Kevin and I watched Wimbers together today. Each of the women's matches drew the following comments from him.

"She has an unfortunate face, doesn't she?"

"Her teeth are rather recessive, don't you think?"

"I couldn't understand what she said, but I know exactly what she meant."

"Pretty little thing isn't she?"

All these comments served to objectify the diverse, exquisite, professional women tennis players. I listened and responded to none of it—out loud—but my mind worked overtime, matching his judgments of them with my own, of him.

Big sigh! It feels better to have released all that. Thank you for bearing with me, HB.

Damian left for Greece, hesitating at the door long enough to punch me gently on the arm with brotherly affection, saying, "Well done, Ju! You've got everything under control." I felt acknowledged. My siblings and I live in such different paradigms—and naturally we each prefer our own. Understanding that makes it relatively easy to accept.

I've been holding you in my heart all day, wondering what you are doing hour-to-hour, hoping the chiropractor worked his magic; and that you got the truck tire fixed; wondering if Sándor arrived, wondering and wondering, and wanting him to have done so, for Anna's sake, and his. I'll find out soon enough. David and Susan are due to arrive there, tomorrow. And my mind is off in New Mexico, again! And that's what is.

Mother is an angel, and I'm so privileged to be supporting her. I wonder if she might be holding on for the 18th, the first anniversary of her surgery. Wondering will get me *nowhere*—and fogs over the stillness within.

More tomorrow, I must get some sleep—I'm exhausted from allowing other realities to spill into my consciousness. Instead of surrendering, I resisted! No wonder I'm exhausted!

Kisses all night, until the morning,
Ju

3rd July
Thursday
9:00 AM

Mother awoke, smiling as usual. I took the warm sponge in with me to "wake up" her face, as she puts it.

When I sat her up to lift her on to the commode, she looked around the room with utter delight, and said, "What a *lovely* room this is. When did I come *here*? I've not stayed in this room before." Then turning to me, she asked quizzically, "Have I?"

Most of her comments and questions emanate from this new reality that comes and goes—some examples from this morning's conversation include,

"They are quiet guests in this hotel, aren't they, dear?" and, "Do the towels have Lincoln Lucifer printed on them?"

Then her caring-mother role emerges through the fog, and she suddenly interjects, "Judith, are you warm enough, dear? You won't catch cold will you?"

Despite having migraine, I slept quite well and ate breakfast with her. After my ablutions, I bathed her. We are waiting for Hazel and the R.N. And the doctor will probably come in today.

It's still gray and overcast. According to the meteorologists it is the worst summer for 100 years.

Wimbers continues to distract me.

I love you. Kisses and hugs,
Ju

◆   ◆   ◆

3rd July
Thursday
11:20 PM
In the sitting room

Hi love,

This was a roller-coasting day for Mother. She had moments of extreme stress, when she was hot, flushed, sweating, and in pain; then hours of tranquil sleep; only to be followed by more agitation, then more stillness and peace.

Tonight, at seven o'clock, after a one and a half hour visit from Ann, Mother elected to listen to the Dick Francis book, *Come Back*. About half way through she called out, somewhat agitated again. She thought it was finished, and said, "… but it didn't make sense." I rewound it to where I thought she might be able to pick up the story again, and left her to listen. But again, she called urgently. She was in pain.

I gave her two painkillers and, while I held her hand, we listened to the end of the story together. I have come to the conclusion that any story with drama and suspense is not helpful to her sense of peace. She was quite agitated. I don't know if it was caused by the story and the pain, or just the story, or just the pain, or something else entirely. Anyway, I switched off the tape and lifted her onto and off the commode. She took her sleeping pills and lay back on her pillows, looking as fragile as a dried leaf.

Smoothing her brow, it felt unusually cool. I whispered quietly that none of us is holding on to her. She wished us both a night of "the best sleep ever." And I chose that moment to tell her about a dream I had last night.

I told her that in my dream I'd seen God waiting for her. I told her that I realized (in the dream) that he was eager to see her, because they'd been such good, good friends, all her life.

"Did ... he ... tell you ... that?" she asked, between small catches of breath, "How wonderful. He knows I'm his friend. I've always loved him."

She pulled me down to her, kissing my lips, and my hands, which she held gently to her face for a moment, and went to sleep saying, "The best sleep ever!"

Tomorrow will bring what it brings.

Continued on 4th July
Friday
9:00 AM
Independence Day in the United States

After using the commode this morning Mother needed more pain medication. She is very short of breath, and clings to my hand, obviously in pain. I stayed with her until the pills took effect—the longest twenty minutes for her. Then, breakfast; she ate a small amount of fruit, drank two cups of tea, and took eleven prescribed pills between seven and eight o'clock. I washed her face and hands, brushed her teeth, and her hair, put Olay on her face, and Chanel #5 on pulse points—all as usual.

She's more confused this morning. No, that's not accurate, she's not confused. Her reality is different. She voices statements, questions, and exclamations that are linked in her mind, but not in mine, not that I could connect them anyway. She's now fast asleep. The pause between her inhaled and exhaled breath is noticeably longer.

While I was bathing Mother, Damian called for the first time since he left forty-eight hours ago. He gave Kevin a contact number and (quite irrationally) I'm *so pissed* at this, he also gave Kevin the phone number of a woman TA knows. It seems this woman has called Mother numerous times, and prior to my arrival insisted on visiting Mother, wanting to check out Mother's health to relay *the truth* to Damian and TA—that was Mother's voiced perception of the woman's visit. TA went to visit this woman last weekend. Mother's generous description of the woman is, "She means well."

Damian's message asked that "… someone give J_____ a call please, to *reassure her*, as *she's so worried* about Mother."

Well, I *lost* it. I looked at Kevin and said, "If Damian wants his g___ d____ friend to know how Mother is, *he can call her from Greece.*" And I slammed upstairs to do my face, and write and complain to you.

This thought process then linked to Sándor. I'm so upset that he hasn't shown up there. I realize I'm causing myself more pain by all these irrational reactive thoughts. It's where I am at this moment. So be it. Surrender, Judith!

And now, having got that out of my system I can be with you again, my love. I do so appreciate your acceptance of these outbursts in my letters, as well as on the phone. They are all part of my own process. I keep gently reminding myself to accept them without judgment.

Kevin has a sore throat and cough. He says, "It's nothing." He doesn't sound very good to me.

Ann called at 8:30 last night, to ask if I'd like to go round to take a break and relax for a bit, particularly in view of "the terrible news." She was referring to the doctor's response to her question of him, yesterday. He told her that Mother could last another four to six weeks. I don't think that's an even vaguely accurate prognosis. Perhaps he said it to comfort Ann, or himself. Anyway, I took a raincheck.

How I long to be with you, to lie with you, to touch you, to feel you close to me, and bask in your sweet, loving, peaceful energy. And I'm here. This is my choice. So be it.

I sent off the request for an additional leave from work. Oh, I've just remembered—I must cancel my flight, right now. My return flight is booked for two hours from now! I'll end this and get it in the mail, pronto.

The sky is blue, the sun is shining. It is another day. And it is now!

Kisses my dearest love, I adore you,
Ju

◆   ◆   ◆

Still 4th July
1:10 PM
In the sitting room,

Hello love,

Much has developed this morning. I think when I ended the last letter Mother was sleeping peacefully, and I needed to call American Airlines. The woman who took my call responded so kindly to me. She said that under the circumstances I'm to hold my ticket, and call them when I know my approximate date of departure to see when they can fit me in on a flight. Today's reservation has now been cancelled. I asked the woman for her name and shall write a letter to the airline, acknowledging her kindness, and genuine compassion.

At about 9:35 AM, I heard Mother moaning. She was in *such* pain, rolling her dear head from side-to-side. The pause following her exhaled breath was so *long*; then, an inhale, gasped in, and more head rolling. I soothed her brow with a cool washcloth, sat her up as much as possible, and settled down next to her on the bed holding her gently. But nothing comforted her.

I called the doctor's office and left a message. Hazel came, *and* Rachel, (they both know the end is near). Hazel asked Mother if she wanted to be bathed. Mother whispered, "No! I'm in too much pain."

So Hazel said she'd just change her pad, and poor Mother had had major diarrhea again. Hazel, bless her, cleaned her all up. Rachel told Mother that she *is* pregnant, but won't know for two more weeks whether her body will be able to retain the embryo. Despite her pain, Mother was so *genuinely* delighted for Rachel, and held both of her hands, *beaming* up at her, telling her how happy she is at her news.

As Hazel and Rachel were leaving, I told them that the doctor told Ann "perhaps four to six weeks more," and Hazel tossed her head in utter scorn, saying, "No way!"

When the doctor arrived at 11:50, Mother was still in pain. He told me to give her 30 mg more of instant-release pain medication, which I did, (this was five hours after the two I'd given her earlier, along with the 90 mg of slow-release at 7:00). Then I fed her some chicken broth, which she seemed to enjoy. By 1:05

the pain was masked, completely; the relief, so absolute, she immediately slipped into a deep sleep.

This afternoon, the district nurse is coming to start the subcutaneous morphine drip, with accompanying syringe-driver. This is supposed to accelerate the pain relief. As long as Mother can swallow, I'll need to continue to give her two sleeping pills at night and the laxative (!) three times a day. The process has accelerated.

I am so weepy thinking about her not being able to swallow. And then I remember to surrender and keep breathing, deeply. Bless dear Mother's heart and soul.

Kevin has his nose buried in a book, and I'm waiting a few minutes before I go to call you. No letter from you again today. Our phone call will nurture me.

Wimbers semi-finals are delayed due to rain. Here though, in the West Country, the sun continues to shine, and I have all three skylights open.

Mother emphasized today that I'm to leave her skylight open, "... no matter what the weather, because that's the way I'm going to leave."

I called Ann to update her, and she said, "I need to avoid all traumas, so I may not come in again," and I encouraged her to take care of herself. Her pain is almost too deep for her to bear.

I'm off to phone you, my love.

9:30 PM

I so enjoyed both our calls today.

The nurses came to set up the new care plan. The computerized syringe-driver dispenses morphine through a very small needle, placed just under the skin on the chest, and is secured there with clear tape to keep it clean and safely in place. A tube goes from the needle to a glass bottle within a holding box, about 6" x 4" x 2". The glass bottle contains morphine, blended with an anti-nausea medication and a sedative—to be time-released over a twenty-four hour period. At, what seem to me, fairly frequent intervals an almost inaudible peeping sound comes from the box, signaling a measured dose being automatically plunged down the tube, through the needle, into Mother's body; the nurses were here for an hour and a half.

Within an hour, after some yogurt and a cup of tea, Mother began to drift off to sleep. She's comfortable again; off in a pain-free world.

Prior to tucking her up for the night she asked for the commode. How very fortunate it is that I can still manage to lift her and place her on it. She was awake enough to balance unaided on the seat—diarrhea again, so, so much. It took a while to clean her up. For her comfort's sake, I hope she remains clean through the night. Despite the doctor's instructions, I withheld the oral laxative.

At about 7:00 PM, to my surprise and amazement, the doctor dropped in to see how Mother is doing. He didn't go up to see her; he just wanted to know how she's doing. Such kindness! Mother was among his first patients when he set up his practice here, twenty-five years ago. This must be challenging for him, watching her dying, and knowing there is nothing he can do to make her well. He always held her in such high regard. But then, I don't know anyone who doesn't.

So good to talk with you and Anna, I do hope the dinner at the café is a fun time for everyone. Sorry to have missed David when I called.

Kevin got supper tonight. I'm grateful. He made toasted crumpets with butter. He's coping in his own way, most of the day just reading quietly.

Ann came in after all, to do her laundry. She says she won't go up to see Mother again, "... now that she has tubes and needles." Seeing them makes her too uncomfortable. She left an hour and a half later, saying, "There's not much point in staying here."

Damian called from Greece, but Mother is electing not to speak with anyone on the phone now. Her sisters also called. So, unless Mother requests to be given the phone again, she has cut herself off from anyone who is not physically here, and has finished with telephones for this lifetime.

How quickly Mother's health has declined. Just last Friday we had the family picnic in her room. She probably doesn't remember it.

Earlier this evening, in her semi-conscious state, she kissed me very gently on the lips, smiling into my eyes with so much love; then trying really hard to focus, she whispered, "I love you, Ju."

My throat constricted, and my heart filled to bursting. I breathed deeply. I was almost overwhelmed by the rush of joy, sadness, gratitude, and loss; tears welled up from the soles of my feet. I breathed deeply into my belly, and allowed the tears to just be there. Mother hasn't called me "Ju" for years. I felt so cherished.

How fortunate I am to have enjoyed so many special visits with her in more recent years—in Carefree, when she came to stay for six weeks; in the Bahamas, where I was working, and where she celebrated her seventy-second birthday; in Northern California, when you and I drove her from San Francisco to the Monterey Peninsula; in Stoke Gabriel, where we strolled along the banks of the River Dart watching a gaggle of children fishing for crabs; at Shapwick, for her 80th birthday celebration, and then last year, at our Sanctuary. Even while she's semi-conscious and dying, her true nature flows forth from her soul—loving, gentle, gracious and, somehow, innocent. How blessed I am to have her as my mother.

It is of the utmost importance to her that she is given the Last Rites. I must time that perfectly for her.

Hazel will be shocked tomorrow to see Mother with a syringe-driver. Well, perhaps not shocked, but disappointed, and saddened. Kevin and I know it's the right course to have taken. When the doctor was here a couple of days ago, he asked us, "Do you think your mother would prefer to be awake, or sleeping?"

"Sleeping," we replied in complete unison, and instantly looked at one another surprised to have agreed on something. And the doctor called his office right away to set up an appointment for the nurses to come in and set up the new care plan. And so it is done.

I need some sleep, more tomorrow.

Kisses, I love you
Ju

HB and Anna at the Sanctuary, on 4th July

Continued on 5th July
Saturday
7:50 AM
Women's Finals at Wimbers

Hi HB,

I was up at 4:30 AM, Mother's breath rattling more loudly on each exhale. I squeezed some drops of water into her mouth, but she didn't wake up enough to open her eyes; I sponged her face with warm water, gently blotted it dry, and left her to sleep.

At 5:00, I changed her pad. It is very challenging to do this with so little physical response from her. She became conscious enough to help a little, by rolling to one side, but I mostly maneuver her body as gently as possible to clean her up, put the new pad in place, and pull up her pants. Perhaps there's an easier way to do it. I might have watched the expert, Hazel, but always leave them to enjoy their time together.

I went back to bed until 6:00, but couldn't sleep, so rose to bathe and wash my hair, and then sponged Mother's face again, and gently brushed her hair. I sat her more upright, hoping to ease her rattling breath. When I asked her if she'd like a cup of tea, she nodded, and whispered, "Yes, please," so I trotted downstairs to make it at 6:40 AM. Kevin was still snoring away on the sofa.

Mother took small sips of tea, and a couple of spoons of apple that I'd stewed yesterday. She managed to swallow the prescribed pills, but I don't think she'll be conscious enough to take them this way tomorrow. I understand that the syringe-driver medication has an accumulative effect, and she'll go deeper and deeper (or higher and higher), then—just leave. What a blessed release for her. Ever since she was diagnosed with chronic leukemia, she's talked longingly of dying. And here we are, twelve years later, and she's not dying of leukemia at all.

Yesterday, the doctor said that Mother's heart and pulse are still really strong. Amazing how some organs can keep going. He also said that whatever portion of her liver is still clear of cancer it is enough to keep processing what it needs to process. So, if her breath-rattle doesn't lead to her lungs filling up, she may still hold on for a while.

Hazel's due in at 10:00; I'll need to change Mother's pad one more time before she arrives.

Kevin's voice has gone down into his boots. It sounds like bronchitis. I encouraged him to take some of my Echinacea; he acceded. It may help.

This morning, I received a lovely note from Eleanor and two lovely letters from my dearest love. Thank you, and thank you. And thank you again, for taking care of dear Ollie for me. I know dogs pine for their primary relationship when they are separated. I'm aware of that feeling.

I was present to you all last night, dining together at the café.

8:35 AM

I just took a break from writing to give Mother another warm-sponge-wash—face and hands—and to smooth on Olay. It is just to nurture her. Her skin really has no need for any further conditioning. It fills my need too, of course, to nurture her in ways with which we have both become familiar over the last six weeks. Her breath is rattling more; she's not able to clear her throat and has insufficient strength, or will, to give a real cough.

HB, I agree with your musing, that at death the energy within the body simply shifts to a new frequency and flows into the infinite energy that is. You and I are on parallel, interdependent paths, both committed to the growth of our consciousness. This act will not split up—we'll always be on the same frequency, whether within or without our form. We are, metaphorically speaking, hand-in-hand, and we will keep on growing, going on together, beyond our physical bodies, when our time comes to leave.

I love you,
Ju

P.S. Hazel came at 8:50 AM, deeply saddened that Mother is now on the syringe-driver, though she's relieved that Mother is pain-free. She says it will be only days now, as Mother "… isn't waiting for anything else. Is she?"

"Only the Last Rites," I said, and went on to tell her that when Mother was in such pain yesterday, she asked me, "Is Damian coming back?"

I replied, "No, he isn't. You said good-bye to him when he left for Greece. Do you remember?"

Hazel seemed pleased at my response, saying that now Mother won't wait for Damian to return.

For the first time, I watched Hazel change Mother's pad, and realized that I do it the same way. I'm just clumsy at it. We both lifted Mother into a higher sitting position, bolstered with many pillows and, for now anyway, the rattle has eased a little. Hazel coached me to position Mother on her side tonight.

Hazel is such a great comfort to Mother, and to me. She said to call her any time if I need any additional help—true kindness. It's 9:40 AM, and it's been such a full morning already—and now to the rest of the day.

I can always use Wimbers to distract me, if need be.

I love you, HB. Kisses,
Ju

◆   ◆   ◆

5th July
Saturday
Noon
Cricket is on

Hello HB,

So many incongruous things occur. For example, the woman living next door—whose back door is at right angles to Mother's front door—knows that Mother is close to death. She's also aware that Mother receives Conservative Party political literature on a weekly basis—because it is dropped in plain view on the mat outside Mother's front door.

This morning, she, Jane, saw me through the open patio door, and beckoned me outside. She called, in a rather strident and imperious tone, "I'm delivering leaflets for the Labor Party candidate. Do give these to your mother," then, as an afterthought, "How is she?"

I flung a sardonic reply over my shoulder as I turned back into the house, "Not interested in voting."

Kevin has been out for a while. He went to post my letter to you and pick up a couple of things at the grocers, then to look for more second-hand books. He has accumulated a pile of eighteen books, all bought since he arrived four weeks ago. I noticed that he's begun to tidy-up his piles of paper, beginning to prepare for his return to Spain.

Today, we have glorious sunshine.

Mother is sleeping. I've placed one of the Walkman ear pieces in one of her ears, so she can hear soothing harp music—if she chooses to listen to it. Now and then, she whispers, "It's lovely," with a simply beautiful smile—but I don't know if she is referring to the harp music, or something else. At other moments, when she moves her lips in inaudible whisperings, I wonder if she is praying.

Ann called again. "Is Mother in a coma yet?"

"No, she's in intermittent, deep sleep … and hazy wakefulness."

"She won't be able to eat any more then." She said, more as a statement than a question.

"Oh, I expect she will," I replied. "She drank fruit juice this morning, and perhaps she'll have a little soup for lunch. And she's drinking plenty of water."

"Nothing solid?"

"No, nothing solid."

And at that, she changed the subject, "I've washed my hair and may come round later."

9:40 PM

I just spoke with you, Anna, and David. It is so comforting to be in touch.

Mother is actively responding to my many-times-whispered, "I love you," and to gentle kisses, and to hand and brow stroking. There is no other comfort of the touching kind available here, to either of us. My siblings show their caring in other ways.

After Mother's gone, and until I can come home, I'll need to continue to nurture myself somehow, and to find a quiet place to grieve in peace and privacy—without becoming self-indulgent. The latter is an easy pitfall. I've begun to grieve long since, of course, and even more deeply since the syringe-driver went in—Mother's advancing absence keenly felt each time my mind drives off into the future.

As I tended Mother's plants earlier, I contemplated on what creates a *full* life, and I think it is *the stillness* in which we can dwell in every moment, even while attending to the necessary structure of everyday life. Conscious stillness generates such peace.

10:00 PM
Dusk

As I walked back from phoning you an hour and a half ago, a brightly-colored hot air balloon, with wicker gondola suspended below, floated silently across the evening sky, and most likely sailed right over the spires of the cathedral, as it was flying in that direction. That is surely a lovely thing to experience, to balloon over the verdant English countryside, in relative silence, just as the sun begins to drop to the horizon, and the shadows lengthen on the surface of the earth below.

Wimbledon will be over tomorrow—we are losing that distraction.

And with the advent of the syringe-driver the hectic daily routine of the last several weeks has abruptly changed. No more commode stops, little oral medication, lighter meal preparation, though the latter is no less frequent.

I think I'm feeling sorry for myself again, allowing the anticipation of loss to overshadow the stillness within and, as it does so, sadness wells up, like the Mississippi River overflowing its banks in a spring thaw. Once I become aware of my mind's self-indulgence the sorry-little-me soon dissolves.

I love you,
Ju

◆   ◆   ◆

6th July
Sunday
8:30 AM

Hello Love,

As Hazel suggested, I managed to position Mother on her left side last night, bolstered with pillows, hoping to drain what might be mucous from her throat. I left her sleeping at 11:00 PM, and went to bed exhausted, falling asleep immediately. I'm still tired this morning.

At 4:50 AM, I awoke to hear Mother moaning. I changed her pad—her urine, a deeper, darker, orange hue. My clumsiness caused her to slide so far down the bed that she lay beached, half-way down the mattress, with her toes over the end, and the bank of pillows beyond the reach of her head. She kept moaning, and whispering to me with such a heartrending, beseeching look, "Help me, Judith!"

As gently as possible, I used all my strength to maneuver her body up to the pillows then covered her. Asking her if she felt pain, she said quietly, "Yes, I feel rotten," and sweeping her limp hand across the coverlet, above her abdomen and liver, she indicated, "It is here … and here." Her jaw clamped shut as she closed her eyes.

I told her I needed her to take two instant-release pain pills, and eventually she managed to swallow them (not without some dread on my part that they'd sit on her tongue, or stick in her throat, and taste terrible if she couldn't swallow).

At 5:30 AM she was still moaning, pain-filled eyes focused inward. I called the district nurse on night duty. By 5:55 she arrived, and immediately depressed the syringe-driver to give Mother an extra dose and, at the same time, instructed me how to administer it. She waited until the additional dose took effect—endless minutes—then together we changed Mother's pad again, and sat her up at the top of the bed on freshly plumped pillows.

I washed Mother's face very gently, brushed her hair and cleaned her partial plate. It was with some difficulty, because she couldn't help, that I managed to reinsert the plate into her mouth. Then I made a pot of tea for the three of us, poured it, and we sat quietly together. Mother wanted to hold her own cup and, somehow, she managed it, (with my hand in close attendance) drinking down a whole steaming cupful, saying after each sip, "Delicious! Delicious!"

As the district nurse left, I quietly asked her how Mother could be so awake today, since she'd been so out of it since the syringe-driver was introduced. She said that Mother's body has adjusted to the medication dose, and she can now tolerate it without being completely sedated.

I translated this to mean that Mother will not necessarily be sleeping, but her pain will be masked—though that's not evident, given this morning. If I need to boost the frequency of the dose I will, but, as directed, I will need to call the day nurse—who comes to refill the glass bottle every twenty-four hours—to come earlier, as the medication will be used up sooner. Mother's resting now, but I don't think she's asleep.

I've just noticed it's a glorious morning, sunny, and bright.

Hazel will be here soon to bathe Mother. I've eaten breakfast, and will finish this letter to get it off to you in the Sunday post.

I'll be happy for Mother when she let's go, and this is over for her.

Kisses, and many gentle hugs,
Ju

◆   ◆   ◆

6ᵗʰ July
8:00 PM

Hi Love,

I want to capture this, her last day, before it's washed away in grief and the practicalities of what comes next.

After breakfast I literally ran to the Presbytery, about five hundred yards up the road. Father Jim came to the door, and I told him of Mother's condition, and added that the Last Rites needed to be administered, immediately. I was gobsmacked by his reply.

"Oh! I'm going to be on a Retreat this week."

"How long will you be away? When are you leaving?"

"I'm leaving this afternoon, until a week from Tuesday."

"Who stands in for you when you're gone?"

"I don't even know that yet. Vincent will tell you."

"Please give me Vincent's phone number. I don't even know his last name!"

At this, he reached for an address book, saying, "Father Barnaby (his predecessor) didn't leave me complete records. I could kill him for that!" This was said with a loud chortle, though the form his language took, surprised me.

I returned quickly to the house. It was 9:40 AM; Hazel was with Mother. I went upstairs to Mother's room. Hazel didn't turn round. She was holding Mother's hand, and said, very quietly. "She said good-bye to me. Didn't you, my dear?"

From Mother's lips came an almost imperceptible, "Yes, Hazel."

Hazel and I worked together to change Mother's pad, and Hazel bathed her. We lifted Mother's limp body back up to the top of the bed, fairly upright. She began moaning again, softly, and her head fell forward. When Hazel asked her if she was in pain, she whispered, "Yes."

This was the first time Mother was unable to hold her head back against the pillows. I boosted the syringe-driver once, and asked Mother if she would like a cup of coffee with Hazel.

She whispered, "Yes, please."

When I took the coffee up on a tray, Hazel pointed out, very unobtrusively, that Mother was cold, her fingers swollen, and her nails darkening. Her circulation was slowing down. I suddenly recalled Anna's voice, telling me, to "... watch for a color change in Gran's nails." I could feel my heart expanding with love, pain, joy, sorrow—all at the same time.

I left Mother and Hazel to spend what I knew would be their last private moments together, and called the day district nurse's number, to have her paged. She called back before Hazel left.

She is a deep-voiced, friendly, cheerful woman whom I'd not met before—Cindy—she tended Mother once or twice, before I arrived. Cindy assured me that she'd get here as soon as possible. I returned to Mother's room, and Hazel said softly, "It won't be long, Judith."

She leaned over and very gently kissed Mother's brow and, with a deeply saddened expression, she quietly left the room.

I stayed with Mother then, sponging her face with warm water, and gently blotting her skin dry. She burped, often. I managed to support her drooping head with a pillow placed by her right shoulder, so she could loll her head to the right, and rest it.

She looked so helpless, her head wobbly, like a newly-hatched bird, and she begun to dribble, seemingly without the necessary reflexes, or enough energy, to swallow. I smoothed cream on her dry lips, and gave her small sips of water, then held her hand and whispered that she had nothing to wait for anymore; it was time to go; no one was holding her back, and that we all wished her a blissful journey, free of her body. Tears rolled silently down my cheeks.

Cindy arrived, and immediately called the on-duty doctor, who prescribed a higher dose of morphine. Cindy instructed me to give Mother two more instant-release pills, if I could get her to swallow them; I did.

It was obvious that Mother was sinking fast, her hands were visibly purpling, her arms, cold and clammy, her face cooling.

Cindy said, very quietly but with a great sense of urgency, "You mentioned that your mother wants the Last Rites. It's time for them, *now*."

Cindy's words jogged me to my senses. I ran down stairs and called the Presbytery; no reply; then, Vincent; no reply again, I left an urgent message on Vincent's machine and turned to Kevin, asking him to run to the Presbytery, to see if Father Jim was still there.

Kevin related later that he knocked repeatedly, and rang the bell three times before Father Jim came to the door; he was eating a sandwich. Kevin told him to come quickly. I think, by then, it must have been close to 12:35 PM. Father Jim asked Kevin if it could wait until one o'clock, because auditors were coming to pick up the parish books.

Kevin told him, "No, it can't wait," and generously offered to wait for the auditors himself, which Father Jim accepted.

The next thing I was aware of was Father Jim bursting through Mother's front door, cheerfully smiling; he climbed the stairs, commenting, "What a lovely day it is."

Cindy asked him to wait a few seconds, while she gave Mother the new, stronger dose of morphine, so she would be pain-free. She spoke to Mother all the while, and I was on the other side of the bed, holding Mother's hand and stroking her hair.

Cindy finished; Father Jim moved in, and began, by saying, "Is anyone else coming? The more the merrier at these things!"

I wondered if I was in a bad movie—then recognized that in his reality this was the most joyous of occasions—a member of his flock, preparing to meet God. Cindy said this was her first attendance at the administration of the Last Rites and asked to stay, which I thought was lovely.

Ann appeared at the bedroom door and, on seeing Mother's state, began to sob uncontrollably, repeatedly whispering, "Poor little Louise, poor little Louise." (She's called Mother by her middle name for several years.) I asked Ann if she could muster some peaceful energy, but she couldn't stop sobbing; I asked her to leave, and she turned on her heel and left the room—I heard much about this later, and the pain my directive caused her.

Father Jim began the Last Rites with several prayers, then he said, "It's usual, at this point, for the person to say their last confession, but she doesn't look like she's going to do that, so, I'll give her absolution."

Mother's eyes were wide open, her head lolling to one side, her pupils dilating as the new dose of morphine took effect. Voicing, "Amen," at the appropriate times, I took Mother's right hand and arm, moving it across her body to make the sign of the cross for her; touching her fingertips to her forehead, to her sternum, to her left shoulder, then to her right; her arm held no resistance at all; it was as light as a fairy's wand.

I bowed my head, and Father Jim took the sacred oils, anointing Mother's forehead and hands. After reciting the Lord's Prayer, he turned to his leatherbound book and read from it, quietly. While he continued murmuring through the ritual of prayer, I raised my eyes, watching his fingers as they moved the red and gold ribbons from one page to the next.

The reading soon came to an end; Father Jim placed his book on the bed then blessed Mother with his hands, saying "In nomine Patris, et Filii, et Spiritus Sancti. Amen." With her hand still resting in mine, Mother closed her eyes and, with a rush of joy, I realized that she was fully aware that she'd received the Last Rites.

Quietly, I thanked Father Jim for coming and, tucking the sacred book under his arm, he nodded, and left the room.

I remained sitting on the edge of Mother's bed, gently stroking her hair, my eyes on her face—at the same time listening to Father Jim, whistling merrily, as he bounced energetically down the stairs. Before his foot could even have found the last tread, Mother frowned; her lips compressed tightly, as though resisting some bitter taste, and she released a great sigh, long and slow—as though relieved of some unbearably heavy burden. Spittle oozed from the corner of her full, soft mouth, and, gently absorbing the moisture with a tissue, I waited for her next breath.

Rather, a sublime expression flooded her face, and her head lolled gently forward onto her chest.

My heart leapt; thudding; pounding; bursting, yet beneath it—I felt a profound stillness. Raising my eyes to the open skylight I heard my voice barely whisper, "She's gone," and knew, in the center of my being, that every vestige of divine energy had flown from Mother's beautiful body. She was gone—into the vastness beyond.

I was vaguely aware of Cindy, quietly stepping forward and feeling for Mother's pulse. Then I heard her voice say, as though from a great distance, "Yes. She's gone."

There was a pause, then Cindy's voice—hardening with authority—punctuated the silence, "What time is it, Judith? You need to record the time."

It was 1:13 PM, Greenwich Mean Time.

Ann came in, her eyes big and round, her hand over her mouth. I looked at her stricken face and said, gently, "She's gone, Ann."

"I thought she'd gone when I came in before! Poor little Louise," then urgently added, "Can you close her eyes? Can you close her mouth?"

At this, Cindy and I removed several pillows, and lifted Mother's body further down the bed to a more gradual incline. I closed Mother's eyelids, then walked across the room to pick out a narrow scarf from her bureau drawer and, when I returned to the bed, Cindy gently held Mother's lower jaw closed as I positioned and tied the scarf in a way that would allow Mother's mouth to set closed.

Ann asked, "Shouldn't her dentures be taken out?"

"No," responded Cindy, "They should be left in, so the face can set properly."

By now, I was sitting quietly by the bedside, holding Mother's hands between my own. It was abundantly clear that all the life energy had left her body. It was absolutely vacant.

Cindy filled out paperwork, asking Ann to witness the removal of the morphine-filled bottle and the flushing of its contents down the toilet. After this, Ann did not return right away.

With that done, Cindy placed a Band-Aid on the place where the needle had been inserted in Mother's chest. Mother's eyelids opened slightly and I freed up one of my hands to gently hold her eyelids closed. Minute-by-minute, as the blood drained away from the upper surface of the body, Mother's skin took on a sallow hue. I sat there, stroking; holding; smoothing, whispering some words of comfort. I remember hearing myself say, "We'll all be alright. We'll be alright."

Cindy was wonderful. She called the doctor on duty to tell him there had been a death; he said he'd be over, to make the official pronouncement. At this point, I stood up and, quite automatically, I crossed Mother's arms across her chest; fingertips resting on the opposite shoulder (like a stone knight on a tomb in a cathedral—as a child I'd thought how comfortable they looked in that position); it seemed the natural thing to do. I then pulled the bedclothes up to her chin. She looked so very beautiful, peaceful, and serene. I stroked her face, and kissed it, many times, very gently.

I heard Cindy say, "When I die I'd like you there. You're so peaceful. I think that really helped your mother leave."

At this, I began to weep, and Cindy came over and patted my shoulder, saying what a lovely lady Mother was, and something about her wonderful sense of humor. Her touch felt intrusive, and my flood gates closed. No doubt to be reopened later.

Ann returned, looked at Mother's body, and said fervently, "I'm so glad to see you got her mouth closed," then cried out, "Why are her eyes opening?"

"It's just gravity," I said, grasping for straws of comfort, not knowing if that made any sense at all.

As soon as Father Jim arrived at the Presbytery, Kevin returned to the house, and I immediately expressed my gratitude to him, for making it possible for Mother to receive the Last Rites. When he saw her vacant body lying there, he looked utterly bereft, and murmured, "Poor Ma," and spun on his heel and left, to be alone with his own grief; he was gone for quite some time.

The on-duty doctor arrived. I'd not met him before. He followed me into Mother's bedroom and quietly went about his business. He lifted Mother's eyelids, shone a light into her eyes, listened to her heart, felt for her pulse, and pronounced her dead.

He instructed me to pick up the death certificate from the office, sometime after noon tomorrow, and indicated that it should be taken to the Registry. He also said to call the undertakers to pick up the body. He left, and Cindy followed.

For over an hour, I sat alone with Mother's body; it was pure peace. With my hand resting lightly on her shoulder, I sat talking to her spirit, tears flowing freely. I took the scarf from around her head. Her lips were slightly parted.

Then I thought about letting people know, and chose to telephone Hazel first; then Mother's sister, Norah. I asked Norah to tell Sarah, her daughter, and her son, David, (who called yesterday for the first time), and Norah's twin, Isabel. Then I called the hotel in Greece, at the number Damian gave Kevin, and left a message for him to call me back; he did so, almost immediately. When I told him Mother had died, he said quietly, "We're orphans now, Ju."

Mother's eyelids partly opened, again, and as I washed her face, hands, and arms, and brushed her hair for the last time, I noticed that her pupils seemed less dilated. Her body was fast chilling.

Just before three o'clock I called the undertakers, and about half an hour later, a white, unmarked van pulled up outside. Two men came to the door and followed me upstairs. One of them instructed me to go to the undertaker's office, tomorrow, with "the paperwork," and then added gently, but firmly, "Now, if you'll leave us, Miss, we'll go and get the stretcher from the van and take care of this by ourselves."

As they left the room, I went to the third drawer down in Mother's bureau, and lifted out the item she'd chosen to be dressed in after her death, the one with the note, reading, "This one, Judith." It is a brand new, full-length, long-sleeved, soft white, cotton nightgown, with buttons from sternum to throat; the neck and cuffs edged with a narrow ruff of broaderie Anglaise. I pulled out the pin that secured the note to the fabric, and tucked the note into my pocket, reflecting on Mother's lifelong determination to look her best—even in death. Then, turning to Mother's body, and as though she could hear me, I said, "You'll look lovely in this."

When the two chaps returned with a stretcher and a body bag, I handed the nightgown to one of them, saying, "This is what my mother wished to be dressed in. Please see to it." They nodded their assent.

I knew I couldn't have changed her gown on my own, and I couldn't bear to strip her body naked with the help of two strange men. So be it.

Leaning over the bed, I kissed Mother's brow one last time and whispered, "Good-bye, Mother," and left to call you, Anna, and David.

Thank you for your support today, HB, and for sharing those moments with me. A much needed heart-to-heart connection. Thank you for listening as I sobbed out my grief in the telephone kiosk—crowds of holiday-makers milling around outside—and for sharing yours; you and I, in a personal bubble of grief, sharing the death of my mother. I'm comforted to know you have Anna and David with you.

Despite the pain of her last morning, Mother's actual moment of death was pain-free and beautiful. She waited for the priest to give her absolution and the Last Rites, and it was only then that she felt complete enough to let go, and she did so, in peace.

I witnessed some of my chattering thoughts, like "… if I'd called Father Jim yesterday, Mother might have avoided today's pain …" but switched that off, immediately. It is as it is.

When I returned from talking with you, Mother's body was gone. I stripped the bed and laundered the linen and towels then bagged all used items—pads, pants, toothbrushes, sponges; anything that was disposable.

I remembered then, that at about 6:00 AM I'd taken out Mother's partial plate, scrubbed it clean, and managed to reinsert it, "Thank you, dear," she'd said, and smiled, gently squeezing my hand. In that moment of recollection, I felt such peace and joy at being able to do that for her—such a small thing.

The unused absorbent pads, the commode—scrubbed clean and disinfected—all the wipes, and creams, and other items the nurses brought in over the weeks, I bagged them all, or placed them to one side—ready to go with the person who comes to pick up the mattress that Mother lay on. That mattress was a blessing; Mother had not one pressure sore.

She was beautiful in life and beautiful in death. I feel so privileged to have supported her in these, her last weeks. Though I feel quite exhausted, I'd do it again tomorrow. There's so much work of a different kind to be done now—all in the next two weeks.

After I called you, I went to the edge of the moat surrounding the Bishop's Palace, next to the cathedral, and sat on the steps across from the bell under the window. Do you remember the bell that the swans ring, each afternoon at 5:00, hoping to be fed?

For fifteen uninterrupted minutes, I gazed at the reflection of the willows overhanging the water—immersed in the stillness of the afternoon and in Mother's death. A child's voice broke the silence, and when I turned, my eyes rested on a small assemblage of flowers growing against a stone wall—blue irises. They seemed to take on the aura of my mother's beauty, her simplicity, elegance, charm, and grace; and I found myself imagining that wherever her spirit is now, there is a great celebration in full swing, and everyone is dancing to *In the Mood,* surely being played by Joe Loss and his big band.

We shall have one this week: a celebration of the life of Enid Louise, born on the 12th September, 1912, and died today, 6th July, 1997; a woman of grace.

I love you,
Ju

5

Partings

7th July
5:55 AM
In bed

Hi Love,

As I awoke, St. Cuthbert's was striking the hour of 4:00 AM. The morning light was flooding dawn into 'my' little bedroom, and I listened for breathing in the next room. Then reality flooded in, and my whole being filled with a sinking, leaden weight, and I turned over, and wept myself to sleep.

At 5:20 I awoke again, and began to consider what needs to be done here before I'll feel complete, and can leave with the knowledge that Ann will have only the executor to deal with over the coming months—that's more than enough work.

At 5:45, Kevin came upstairs to shave. We exchanged good mornings, and when he spoke I realized for the first time, that since his arrival he has been whispering. He looked around 'my' bedroom door, and said, "You can stay in bed all day, Ju. If you like."

Touched by his generosity, I smiled, recognizing his offer as a family gesture of care. I told him I appreciated it but would get up shortly, and asked him to watch for the postman, who might bring me a parcel containing tea—from my beloved.

He then asked, if, when I spoke with Anna yesterday, she'd mentioned the requested visitation from Mother—I'd told him of Anna's request of her Gran—and told him I hadn't heard yet.

I shall get up now, and change my bed linen. I washed Kevin's sheets yesterday.

There's much to do. One of which is sorting out Mother's remaining clothes: three assorted-weight coats; her two favorite outfits; her size 4 shoes, and her hats.

Then her bureau must be emptied, with its five drawers containing nightgowns, scarves, underwear, gloves, and perhaps four or five sweaters. Not much really; a lesson to be learned from her—to live simply.

First, I want a long, hot bathe. Later, I'll need to take Mother's birth and marriage certificates, her pension and medical cards, and other legal papers of identification, and go to the Registry.

I think I'll begin this day again, in this moment, and make it a happy one, filled with love, in Mother's memory.

I love you,
Ju

◆   ◆   ◆

7th July
10:55 PM
In the bedroom

Dear HB,

This is a short note.

I made my flight plans. I'll be home on the 18th, at 5:00 PM. I called my manager, Nicole, to request the week of the 21st off. She granted it, and I must return to work on the 28th.

So good to talk with you, today, and to know you are collectively erecting the tipi. It will be a marvelous addition to the garden.

Today has been a document collection and delivery day. Kevin fetched the Notice of Death, plus the Notice to Informant from the doctor's office. He took those, along with Mother's birth and marriage certificates, to the Registry. In exchange for these, he obtained ten copies of the Death Certificate—for £30—and a form to take to the Social Services office to stop the direct deposit of Mother's pension.

Ann and I went together to the bank, to freeze Mother's account. We then made appointments with local realtors, for two evaluations of Mother's house, for Tuesday and Thursday.

Taking an additional form that Kevin brought back from the Registry, I went to the undertaker's office to arrange for the cremation. I also completed making the funeral arrangements with the church, for Friday the 11th, and finalized the wording of Mother's obituary with the date of death. The latter, and the acknowledgements due to all Mother's caregivers, and to those who are sending messages of sympathy, will be printed in the local newspaper next week. Somehow I made time to eat lunch and supper.

I took the sheepskin mattress pad and bed cover off Mother's bed and washed them at the Laundromat; both items look like new. I also took already-laundered-at-home clothes, and dried them at the Laundromat. Now there is time available, to walk the quarter mile, load the machine, wait while it all dries and walk back, without hurry.

A wonderful letter came from you today. Thank you, HB.

The doctor, Hazel, Pauline (one of the RNs), and Paul, came to the house to express care for the living, and love for the departed—such thoughtfulness.

Damian called, to ask me to make a booking at the B & B for him and TA, for Thursday night.

Can you tell I'm focusing on getting things done? Much, much more to do tomorrow, including buying another of these writing pads.

Kisses,
Ju

◆   ◆   ◆

8th July
1:00 PM

Hi Love,

If I leave here without completely losing my mind, to violence or hysterics, it will be a *miracle*. I need a miracle.

Here are some completely foolish annoyances that my mind is creating and, in so doing, pulling my attention headlong, out of the present: even though I am fully aware that we are all grieving Mother's loss, my mind's current grip is so strong that I'm reacting to what is going on around me, instead of choosing my responses. For example, Kevin named some Prince, with a very long name, which he must have practiced for years to pronounce correctly, and said, "He told me I am the next Buddha!" He then went on to name another famous chap, and said, "He said I am a genius. I don't know why he said that."

I almost broke up at the shocking reaction that my mind immediately concocted, but didn't voice, which was, "It must have been in a past life," and so on, and on, and on, and on.

The pained, sad-little-Judith within notices that Ann appears to be finding fault with what I'm doing, or how I'm doing it. When I said something about cost, which I don't recall now, she asked, "Are you trying to save Mother's money, so you get more?"

I instantly reacted, saying, "If you *must* continue to misinterpret everything I say, so *be* it."

She quickly retorted, "Are you getting aggressive with me?"

"Yes." I almost shouted!

"Then, so am I," came her swift reply, and she lapsed into a stony silence.

And so here we are, Mother's adult daughters, squabbling like pre-teens. Our grief is showing up in many disguises. I keep breathing and letting go, continuing with the tasks at hand, wanting to leave Ann with nothing else but the lengthy task of dealing with the executor.

The temperature is forecast to reach 81°F today and, as the sun is shining out of a clear blue sky and the humidity is rising, it might just rise to that, later.

9:30 PM
Same day

Well, I spilled out my mind's entire bucket of rotten eggs to you on the phone. Thank you for the opportunity to crack them all open and flush them away. Your willingness to listen deeply—without collusion or judgment—gives me pure joy and is such a comfort.

After we spoke this afternoon, I took your sage advice to chill out at the Good Earth restaurant, and enjoyed a piece of toasted garlic bread, and a glass of wine.

Then, as you also suggested, I did indeed find a secretarial service in the village, and delivered the eulogy to be typed up and have copies made. Thanks for such helpful suggestions.

I strolled around the market place while waiting for the document to be finished, then picked up the death announcements, which I've now addressed, and have ready for the mail tomorrow—a good job done.

Many tasks completed today, too numerous to list here, or even remember, as they are now crossed off the list. I have another list of twenty-five more things to be done before I leave, and can only imagine that when those are done there will be twenty-five more to take their place.

I cancelled the hotel booked at Gatwick for the 17th, and reserved a taxi to pick me up at Mother's house at 5:00 AM, on the 18th. That extra night, alone in her house, will offer the stillness I need, to leave here in a conscious way.

For the first time since Sunday I went round to Ann's, and she talked about Mother's death in detail, which she clearly needed to do. I supported her without interruption, as you had done for me on the phone. Ann has had no opportunity to talk about it until today, and I felt able and willing to put aside my head full of things that must get done, and my own grief, and be there for her, fully.

Rachel came in to get closure. She is indeed pregnant and is cautiously happy about it. She said the doctors will check her again in three weeks, to see how she's doing. After I return home I intend to stay in touch with Rachel and Hazel. I have such love and regard for them both.

Kevin made supper. I ate five toasted crumpets accompanied by a glass of ale: comfort food.

It's 9:50 PM. I called you, but no reply. You must be on your way to the airport with Anna and family; the reunion is over—*sans moi*, and absent Sándor.

Norah called, she and Sarah will be here for the funeral; they arrive tomorrow.

◆   ◆   ◆

9th July
10:50 PM

Hello my love,

I just got off the phone with you; I can hear we are both ready to be together again.

It's been a long day, starting at 6:00 AM and ending at 9:00 PM. The focus of today was on sorting and packing Mother's remaining clothes. The Hospice Charity shop will be glad of them.

With that done, I scrubbed the wardrobe and bureau in Mother's room, as well as the wardrobe and bureau in 'my' room. I also emptied the chest at the top of the stairs, and Mother's desk, and both her file boxes. The contents of the latter will go to the executor.

Tomorrow, I plan to clean out the utility room, and the kitchen cabinets. It will take most of the day. A third realtor is coming, at noon, to do the last evaluation of the house.

Damian, by his absence, is lagging behind the rest of us, in the process, and I imagine it may be harder for him, as he's no opportunity to get any closure, as we have, being here each day. It may help him a little this weekend, when all four siblings are together, and we plan to empty the chest in the sitting room; it contains family photos, diaries, and other personal items of Mother's.

By then, we will also have seen the executor, and will know if the portable items that Mother bequeathed to each of us, and others, can be packed up for removal. Kevin is helping me to take items that belong to Ann, to her home. Thank goodness her home is in the main house and not miles away.

Tomorrow, there is so much to get done, and I have to steel myself for the funeral, we have the family script to uphold—no public tears.

A letter arrived from Sándor, for Mother.

I love you sweetheart—how wonderful to know we will have nine days together, before I resume work.

I love you,
Ju

◆   ◆   ◆

Sándor's letter to his grandmother, which arrived after her death, with his permission, reads:

"Dear Gran,

I've wanted to write to you for a long time. I've always thought it didn't matter to you whether you got letters from me or not, and I think that's because our family is so spread out, all doing our own thing.

Family, in the traditional sense, has never been very much present to me, but I know as well as anyone else that in our family, at any moment, any family member would be welcome in any one of our homes. If not out of love, it would be out of the sheer "Ah!" of being in the presence of a blood relative.

We truly do have an extraordinary family. I call us "enlightened gypsies," traveling to the corners of the earth, creating our own lives, and making a difference in the lives of our families, friends, and communities. That's who you have been for me, an elegant, enlightened gypsy.

I say, you mastered elegance in your life. Even today, I'll bet you are dealing with your health elegantly. Who you are to me is an extraordinary human being.

I honor you as my friend, and most of all, I honor you as my grandmother. I want you to know that you are grand to me, you are a grand mother. It has been an honor and privilege to be in your life.

Thank you for contributing to my life and allowing me to contribute to you. Because of you, I was born. Because of you, I have a life that I love. Every day I wake up, I am present to the joy of being alive.

Thank you for bringing my mother into this world. Thank you for teaching her to be an extraordinary mother. Thank you for teaching her the distinction of living life to its fullest, of being a woman of honor, love, and integrity.

There is a quote by George Bernard Shaw, it goes something like this: "I am of the opinion that my life belongs to the whole community, that life is this splendid torch, and my job is to let it burn brightly, for future generations to see."

Grandmother, I saw your torch, and I will carry it with honor, for all generations to see.

I love you,
Sándor"

◆   ◆   ◆

11th July
7:10 AM

This is one of the endless days in which to celebrate Mother's life—the day of the Requiem Mass and the cremation.

Hi Love,

It's 7:10 AM—two hours before I leave for the church. Mother would be as pleased and satisfied as I am with all that's been accomplished this week. There are a few more things to get done, but today must be met first.

While I was out with Norah last night, Damian and TA arrived at the house. I found them, sitting quietly with Kevin, drinking together in the twilight of the smoke-filled sitting room; no lights were on.

I feel like an emotional dishrag this morning and have to keep refocusing on this day being to honor Mother's life. With all that I feel about her loss, my outward behavior needs to align with what needs to be attended to, rather than allowing my tears to flow—just at the thought of the funeral itself!

Cindy, the R.N., who was with us when Mother died, called to say how much she appreciated the clock that Ann and I delivered to her office, earlier this week—Mother had instructed us to give it to her. Cindy said, "I will always treasure it." She also said that she will look at death differently, now that she knows it can be peaceful and beautiful. She will touch many lives with that awareness—a perfect ripple effect from Mother.

It is a beautiful day! Sunny, clear, and warm, already. The swifts are flying high today; the humidity must be low.

In Mother's bedroom there is a single rose, a gift to her from Paul's garden. He brought it to her about five days before she died, when it was still a tightly closed bud, and by Sunday, when she died, it was fully open. I've kept it in its bud vase, by Mother's bed. It is a dry husk now, yet no petals have fallen. I imagine they will fall while we are at the crematorium, just as Mother's body is consumed in the flames, the last visible vestige of life in her room, gone. Yesterday, Ann wanted to throw the rose away, and I vehemently said, "No!" as I'm using it symbolically each day, to let go, little by little.

More later,

7:15 PM
Twelve hours on

What a long, long day this has been. I got to the church at 9:00, just as the coffin was being wheeled in. Dr. Trafford was still vacuuming the carpet in front of the altar.

Damian, Kevin, and I determined that none of us could read the eulogy with any degree of composure, which Mother would definitely have wanted. So I asked Dr. Trafford if he would read it. He said he would be honored, and I thankfully placed the type written pages in his hands.

Then the Bishop himself arrived, from Taunton. (Father Jim is still away on Retreat.) We were all introduced. The Bishop was dressed in the ritual purple surplice, worn when saying the Requiem Mass.

The family members occupied the two front, right hand pews; Damian, TA, and Norah, in the front pew; Kevin, Sarah, and I, behind them.

Every pew behind us was occupied with two or more people. I recognized a few of Mother's friends, and imagined that all others were parishioners who knew her, and were attending daily Mass as usual.

The casket rested on a wheeled-trolley on the altar, the narrow end pointing towards the door. Our flowers, in the shape of a cross and quite beautiful, adorned the lid of the casket. A white candle, to the left of the casket, burned brightly in a five-foot-tall brass holder. I'd been forewarned—I forget by whom—that there was a wedding in the church, yesterday, and no one had been available to remove the wedding flowers. Thus, fastened at the center-aisle-end of each pew was a fresh, white bouquet, and on the entry steps to the altar, two enormous, white, floral arrangements in vases, on stands. They lent a cheerful air to this celebration of Mother's life—sorry Mother, you had flowers after all!

In order to manage my emotions the way I knew Mother would have preferred, I remained present, aware that this, her funeral, is a formal ritual conducted by her church. Mother's energy was in no sense present. Having sat with her body for over an hour on Sunday, I was fully aware that her coffin contained only the lovely temple that had housed her spirit, and that temple had served its purpose.

The Mass began at 9:30, said by the Bishop. He emphasized the Beatitudes—and I smiled to myself when he mentioned "Blessed are the Meek."

Dr. Trafford read the eulogy with eyes tearing. I didn't know if it was from their usual rheumy condition, or emotion. Perhaps it was both, he was fond of Mother.

Communion was taken by many in attendance, but by none of us.

The Mass ended at 10.00, when the Bishop took the aspergillum—a perforated ball at the end of a short handle—and dispensed holy water the length of the casket; as he said the last "Amen," he beckoned the pall-bearers, who walked silently up the center aisle, took their positions beside the coffin, and solemnly wheeled it out.

As the family members filed passed the occupied pews—Damian, TA, and Norah, followed by Kevin and I—I kept my eyes on the coffin, with our cross of white flowers on top, as it was being loaded into the waiting hearse.

Outside, we were received by Mother's friends with tearful sympathies and handshakes, and nods of condolence from others who were at the Mass. Hazel and Wendy were there, as was Paul.

A fellow-parishioner (and neighbor) of Mother's came over as we were getting into the limousine. Mary, over 80, is a staunch Catholic and a gentle soul—every month, for the past year, she kindly brought Mother the parish newsletter. Reaching inside the open limousine window and firmly grasping my hand, she said, "Judith, your mother was such a wonderful woman. I can't be sad today. I'm just *filled* with joy for her," and she beamed, her face alight with fervor. I found this quite wondrous and lovely.

We drove towards Haycombe and the crematorium. Along the entire route, the countryside was shrouded in mist with filtered rays of sunlight streaming through leafy boughs. It seemed most appropriate for the occasion. Norah and Damian chatted most of the way, while Kevin and I rode in silence.

When we arrived at the crematorium, Father Barnaby—the priest who served in the parish prior to Father Jim—met us at the entrance and led us inside; we took our places in the front pew. Mother was very fond of Father Barnaby.

The entire cremation service took all of ten minutes: to place the coffin, recite the prayers, splash holy water—this time from a plastic squeeze bottle! Then the priest returned to the pulpit and reached for a hidden button; curtains closed around the coffin, and with an audible swoosh, it was lowered away. We said a collective, "Amen," and in keeping with Mother's wishes and our enculturation, not a tear was shed.

Outside, our cross of flowers lay on the grass in front of a printed card, which was inserted into a metal frame with a spike skewered into the soil. We hesitated here for a while, absorbing the words on the card, "In Memory of Enid Louise____" then Damian lit up a Gauloise, and strolled away to be alone. The rest of us stood about, in the silence of our own thoughts.

When Damian rejoined us we were driven back to Mother's house, where Kevin and I changed from our funeral clothes into something more casual. Damian, already comfortable in an open-necked shirt, pants, and sandals, went ahead to hold a table for us in the courtyard of the City Arms.

I went round to Ann's to invite her to join us for lunch, but she declined; her drapes and shutters were closed. She is in deep, private, mourning, expressing her love for Mother in the way that is best for her. We arranged to meet later for our appointment with Mother's executor.

So it was just my brothers and I, and our aunt and cousin, who had lunch together. We ate well enough and toasted Mother, delighting in sharing little stories about her that mostly began with, "Do you remember when ..." or "Did you ever hear about the time ..." and so on.

As we sipped one last glass of wine, Ann arrived, which signaled Sarah to say her good-byes, and Norah to have some time alone. Those of us left gathered our belongings, and trooped off to the executor's office for the reading of Mother's Last Will and Testament, and to learn about the next steps in the process of its execution.

Norah rejoined us at Mother's house at 5:00, and I made a help-yourself-buffet-supper, though Ann could not bring herself to stay for it; she left quietly. The rest of us soon ate our fill and the conversation came to a faltering halt.

I walked Norah up the road, to the B & B where she is staying, and came to call you for the second time.

The funeral is over. Damian and TA said their good-byes and left for the B & B. They depart early in the morning to catch their flight home.

By Thursday, I expect to have finished taking inventory of what remains of Mother's household effects and, after putting an estimated value on everything, I shall deliver the numbers to the executor for him to add them to the value of Mother's estate. Then I am leaving for home and my love, for a week of rest, and to get to know you anew.

Despite the events of the day, I feel emotionally grounded right now, and am fully prepared to scatter Mother's ashes at the Garden of Remembrance, which is within a short walking distance of her home. I remember taking you there, to visit my father's plaque. Do you remember the small, walled garden designated for Roman Catholics? It's within the Protestant cemetery on the road to our favorite B & B.

At Mother's request, I'm bringing home some of her ashes to our Sanctuary, to scatter them there. Shirley, at the undertaker's office, is seeing to it that they are boxed and labeled correctly—in case my luggage gets searched at Customs. When Mother asked me to take some of her ashes home, she emphasized her wishes, saying, "If you *ever* leave the Sanctuary, take me with you, wherever you go."

So I will need to place her ashes in such a way that they can be easily retrieved, should the need arise.

My apologies for being so wound up on the phone earlier.

I love you, kisses,
Ju

◆   ◆   ◆

12th July
9:45 PM

Hello dear HB,

Today felt very long, supporting my brothers choosing some mementos and cajoling Ann to have her choices carried round to her home. Her temporary resistance to receiving them is only because she doesn't know where she'll put them, but they must be cleared from Mother's house. I am bringing a few small items home with me.

There are five more days and nights before I leave to be with you; it feels good to say that.

Continued on 13th July
9:20 PM

The last two days have been spent totally absorbed in wrapping up Mother's house. Kevin and I delivered the last of the boxes to Ann. I've just packed some of Mother's paintings, which Mother wanted Anna to have.

There is much more to do tomorrow, the most important of which is scattering dear Mother's ashes.

Sorry to be so short tempered on both the calls I made to you today. I'm clearly suppressing my welling sadness, in order to get all these emotionally-charged tasks done properly, before I leave.

I invited Ann to come with me to scatter Mother's ashes in the Garden of Remembrance, but she quickly declined, saying, "No, no, I'm too exhausted."

Next I invited Kevin to join me, and he said noncommittally, "We'll see!"

I pressed him further, "Are you indifferent about it?"

"Yes, I am."

"Then, I'll go alone."

To which he immediately replied, "Oh, I'll come with you," in a tone that implied he was doing me a favor. His reality eludes me. Perhaps he felt squeamish about it, I don't know, and I didn't need to pursue it.

Soon after this exchange we left together to walk to the cemetery. The sidewalk is too narrow to stay abreast, so I went ahead, the ashes in a cardboard box held to my chest, with both hands—safeguarding Mother's remains.

The Garden of Remembrance, designated for the local Roman Catholic community, is no more than six hundred square feet, and is contained within a four-sided, four to five feet high, flat-topped, weathered wall, built of locally quarried stone. A fairly wide opening in one side serves as the entrance. The garden is designed simply, with a centered, circular, flower bed, which is populated with rose bushes, creamy-yellow heads, tinged with pink—the Peace rose; Mother's favorite. The rest of the area is a lawn of sweet-smelling, freshly-mown grass, extending to the wall. The memorial plaques are secured on the outside vertical surface of the wall.

When Kevin and I arrived, our cross of flowers was immediately apparent, lying on the grass—thanks to someone from the undertaker's office.

I began by placing the box on top of the wall; then opened it up. The ashes were the palest gray, fine and dense, with fragments of larger granules. I took a handful of the soft dust and began to sift it through my fingers, letting it fall around the rose bushes and onto the grass, saying, "Good-bye, Mother. Good-bye, Mother." Strolling quietly and slowly, I continued this way, scattering handful after handful within this lovely, peaceful garden. At one moment, the breeze lifted, and motes were blown from my hand, floating up above the wall, and disappearing into the sky. I was reminded of the name that Mother gave the Nature Conservancy magazine's Grand Prize photograph—*Into the Silence.*

I continued to let go, let go, let go, and let go; surrendering to the inevitability of the moment, and dwelling in my love for Mother. Kevin chose to scatter the ashes at the base of a majestic yew tree outside the walled Garden. He said, "I think Mother will like the view from this spot." I'm glad he joined me.

We walked back in silence, and though I had done my best to wipe it all off, vestiges of ash still clung to my right hand and arm, right up to the elbow. When we reached the house I discarded the packaging and rinsed myself off, bidding farewell to the residue of Mother's physical body, washing away down the drain.

Within fifteen minutes Ann came round, regretting that she'd not come with us. I'm so sorry she missed it. It might have provided more closure for her, and perhaps even assuaged her pain a little.

A call came from Paris. Damian and TA's plane is delayed there, overnight.

Love you sweetheart, hugs and kisses,
Ju

◆   ◆   ◆

15th July
8:10 AM

Up at 5:00 AM, I bathed and shampooed. Kevin's alarm rang at 5:30 and I heard him making his breakfast. He brought me up a cup of tea—that's twice; I'm grateful.

He's done a fine job squeezing everything he's taking back into an old, many-pocketed hold-all that we found in Mother's attic. That hold-all and his little grip bag are bulging at the seams. An additional shopping bag, with short handles, contains a pork pie, cheese, a loaf of bread (to eat en route), packages of frozen bacon, tongue, smoked mackerel, and a book.

To make it easier to carry, Kevin threaded an umbrella through the shopping bag handles and, when he felt quite ready to leave, he hoisted up the latter in one hand, and the hold-all in the other. Then he and I—I was loaded down with the little grip bag, and my father's horse-racing binoculars, which Mother gave him—set off for the bus station, where he was to catch the 6:30 AM, to Victoria.

Kevin's luggage was so heavy he needed to rest several times during the normally five minute walk, to the extent that he arrived there fifteen minutes after me. All those books he bought weighed a ton! I cannot guess what he'll choose to discard if he's asked by the airline to pay excess baggage fees.

Just before boarding the bus, Kevin leant towards me, and we kissed each other on both cheeks; then his parting question came, "Will you come back to England, ever?"

I looked at him, and said, "You already know the answer to that."

Then, as he stepped up into the bus, he hesitated for a moment, turned back to me, and said, "Well Ju, I could have done it *all* without you—but perhaps not quite so well." All said with a twinkle in his eyes and an acknowledging smile.

Returning his smile, I replied, "I'm sure both statements are correct," then added, "Stay in touch—if you want to."

And he was gone.

I returned to the house to find a card from Anna, and two letters from you—one marked "Penultimate" and another "Ultimate". Thank you, sweetheart.

Norah called, to thank me for the ornaments, sent on Mother's behalf to her and Isabel, and to inform me she now has a new role in the family, "… as the eldest sister." She went on to say that her new responsibilities will be taken very seriously, "… now that Enid's gone," and named these as "… calling Ann regularly, and remembering all your birthdays." She then proceeded to ask me for everyone's correct birth date, address, and phone number. After noting them down and repeating them back, she wished me a safe journey home.

Today, I'll be washing and polishing the kitchen floor, doing some laundry, and mailing the last of Mother's paintings bequeathed to Anna.

Before he left this morning, Kevin spoke very lovingly of Mother, saying he'll miss her very much. I commented on his cough and congestion, and he said, "I've never had this before."

I offered that, in some paradigms, the root cause of respiratory symptoms is "… unspoken words, and unshed tears," and suggested that he might have bronchitis.

"Oh," came his reply, and nothing more was said.

There is much to do before I leave to be with you. It will all be timed to perfection, with nothing left undone—that I can do.

All my love to you, kisses,
Ju

◆   ◆   ◆

16th July
3:10 PM

Hi HB,

This is the fifty-first day of my stay here.

This will be a two-part letter: today's news, and up to lunch time tomorrow, or soon after.

This morning I took the mantle clock to Father Jim at the Presbytery. I hoped that it might find a home there. It was a wedding present to my parents and has always stood on the mantle, or on a desk, in each of their homes. Instead of the Presbytery, Father Jim said he'd like it for the Sacristy at the parish church, where my parents were parishioners, and where both their funeral services were conducted. For some obscure reason I felt really moved by this, and walking back to the house I became all weepy.

Lots of chores completed today, the Inventory of Household Effects, the Accounting for Cash; the list of Donations of Goods given to the Charity Shop. These official documents have now been delivered to the executor's office; I made copies for my siblings.

Continued on the 17th July

Up at 6:00 AM, when I loaded the washing machine with the last of the linen. Tonight, I'll use Ann's sleeping bag and, at 4:00 AM, it will be put back in the utility room with several other small items that are still a part of Mother's household effects. These are slated for auction, eventually.

A few more things to do—leave a new toilet roll and a hand towel in the bathroom, for use by prospective house buyers; buy the local weekly paper to get copies of the acknowledgements; take the vacuum cleaner and phone to Ann—the phone service will be cut off tomorrow; turn the hot water heater off in the morning; give the dark oak furniture one last polish—and all that I can do will be finished. It feels very thorough and complete, and I find I want to tell Mother about it, and hear her say, "Thanks, Ju!" Such is my ego's need for acknowledgement!

The carpets are spotless—like new. The shampooing was completed yesterday, and last night I replaced all the furniture. I've a few errands to do before coming back to finish last-minute packing; that is, after I've taken the laundry to be dried at the Laundromat.

My deepest gratitude to you, HB, for supporting my presence here—with unconditional love, with letters, with Good Earth tea; with care for two of my children and their loved ones at their reunion; with care for our Sanctuary, and golden Ollie; and you did all this while going through the loss of your own dear mother. Dearest HB, I thank you, endlessly, and acknowledge you—the most generous spirit I know, and the dearest of friends.

I love you,
Ju

◆   ◆   ◆

17th July
8:30 PM
In the sleeping bag in 'my' bedroom

Hi Love:

Just before 6:00 PM this evening, I took the last of the bread from the kitchen, hoping to feed the swans at the moat. And there they were, by the steps close to the Bishop's Gate, gliding in pure silence, with such grace—a beautiful pen and cob, with three, fluffy cygnets.

Instantly, the Nature Conservancy magazine's winning photograph flashed into my mind. Did I share the subject of the photo with you? It is an image of Trumpeter Swans, lifting off calm waters; and there, on this late summer afternoon in the tranquility of the English countryside, beside the moat where Mother so often strolled with my father, I felt my mother's energy dancing around and within me, and a deep sense of peace and stillness filled my being. Pure joy!

On my way back, I spotted Father Jim digging in a corner of the Presbytery garden. I stopped, and called out to him, "Father Jim, which flowers do you like to grow? My mother couldn't remember what you told her, and it will give me closure to know."

He stood up, resting a foot on his spade, and called back, "Delphiniums, and hollyhocks," and as I waved my thanks, he returned to the pleasures of tending his garden.

At 7:00 PM, I delivered the phone and the vacuum to Ann, and invited her to join me at the City Arms for supper. It was a somber meal.

With our arms linked, we strolled back to her front door, where I promised to call her this weekend. We exchanged gentle hugs, kisses on both cheeks, and whispered good-byes, and as she climbed the steps to her front door I raised my hand in farewell, and she too was gone.

◆   ◆   ◆

18th July
10:30 AM at Gatwick
Hoping to catch the post here, before my flight takes off

It is one year exactly since Mother's surgery. What impeccable timing!

I was up at 3:45 AM, feeling very weepy and tired. I bathed, put the trash out by the curbside, and my luggage out on the patio. With a flourish, I gave the kitchen sink and countertops a final shine.

Then, for the last time, I walked through Mother's home. In each room, I invoked a blessing, looking or turning in the appropriate direction as I called out:

"From the Father above
From the Mother below
From the East
From the South
From the West
From the North
May blessings be upon this place;
And on all who have dwelled,
And will dwell, here,
May peace be with you."

I entered Mother's bedroom last, and, when I'd finished the invocation, I stood silently for a moment. Then, looking up through the skylight, I held my arms out, wide, and spread open my hands, and called out, "Good-bye, Mother. I'll carry your love with me, wherever I go."

Allowing my tears to flow again, I locked myself out and placed the keys in an envelope addressed to Ann; sealing it, I walked the short distance to her front door and slipped the envelope through her letter box. Then, returning to Mother's front gate, I waited, my luggage at my feet, listening to the gulls wheeling above St. Cuthbert's spire, their plaintive cries echoing my heart.

The taxi drew up, and the driver opened the trunk and quickly loaded the luggage. And I was gone—never to return to that silent, empty house.

See you soon my love,
Ju

Afterword

Rachel delivered a beautiful baby boy, George, on March 26th of the following year, since then, George has been joined by a sister, Rosie.

Anna recounts that at 1:30 AM on the 7th July, something drew her from her bed and, disturbing no one, she slipped quietly from the Sanctuary going beyond the courtyard to the wild flower garden. Reaching the perimeter of the property, she stood motionless, facing the distant mesas in the warm, still silence of the starry night. She listened. A light breeze caressed her face and she became aware of a gentle presence. Though she saw no one, tears of joy spilled down her cheeks. She has no doubt that, as requested, her grandmother stopped by. When I called Kevin to relay Anna's experience, he chuckled delightedly, murmuring, "Good for Ma!"

Soon after he returned home to Spain, Kevin wrote to me, delighted that the airlines did not charge him excess baggage fees. Though exhausted, he arrived home safely, with the contents of his luggage intact. Despite being diagnosed with a serious case of bronchitis, he immediately resumed his teaching role, tutoring his students in the proper use of the English language.

And what of the family photographs Mother imagined we'd fight over? On the day of the cremation, I asked my siblings if I could take home Mother's old and battered family albums, together with the new ones she'd completed during the year prior to her death. I promised to share the photos fairly among us. My siblings agreed and, before we parted, they identified their favorite images of Mother, and I made note of their preferences. With good intentions, I promised to complete the photo distribution by the end of that year; however, it was three years later when I hand-carried a completed album to each of them—to Damian in France, Kevin in Spain, and Ann in England. It was a labor of love and they were appreciative.

Infrequently, Damian has returned to England to see TA's family. He has visited Ann on at least one of those occasions.

Though Kevin remains in touch with Ann, via occasional letters and infrequent phone calls, he has not returned.

Ann and I continue to chat on the phone twice a week, and each year we take a vacation together, usually in England.

I am still in touch with Hazel and Rachel.

HB and I have moved eight times since Mother died and, true to her wishes, her ashes were retrieved from their place of rest at the Sanctuary and are taken with us, wherever we go.

◆   ◆   ◆

During those cherished weeks with my mother, the source of strength from which I drew filled me with wonder, as it does now.

That source—from which grace arises—is infinite stillness, allowing a peaceful acceptance of what is. Without awareness of that stillness, I could not have been in service to my mother in the way that she wanted, and needed.

And today, as every day, that infinite stillness resides within—as it does in all of us; and from it, I continue to observe the chattering of my mind and the flexing of my ego—sometimes with great amusement—and, when I remember to attach no importance to either, life is transformed.

About the Author

Judith M. Ashley enjoyed a twenty-five-year career as a human resources consultant working with two American high-tech corporations and serving her clients in North America, Malaysia, the Middle East, and Europe. She lives in New England with her husband, HB, with whom she continues to weave a life of joy.

http://www.judithashley.com
Email: hbnju@aol.com

978-0-595-68900-2
0-595-68900-0

Printed in the United States
88067LV00007B/15/A